RULES FOR PRAYER

by

William O. Paulsell

Paulist Press
New York/Mahwah, N.J.

Copyright © 1993 by William O. Paulsell

All rights reserved. No part of this book may be reproduced or transmitted in any form or by any means, electronic or mechanical, including photocopying, recording or by any information storage and retrieval system without permission in writing from the Publisher.

Library of Congress Cataloging-in-Publication Data

Paulsell, William O.
     Rules for Prayer/by William O. Paulsell.
       p.   cm.
     Includes bibliographical references.
     ISBN-0-8091-3410-1
     1. Prayer—Christianity. 2. Spiritual Life—Christianity.
     I. Title.
BV215.P38   1993   93-4387
248.3'2—dc20   CIP

Published by Paulist Press
997 Macarthur Boulevard
Mahwah, New Jersey 07430

Printed and bound in the United States of America

TABLE OF CONTENTS

This book is dedicated to the memory of

ARTHUR D. WENGER

whose high standards and personal discipline

were an inspiration.

INTRODUCTION

Over the years, in many retreats and conferences, people have asked me how to develop a more serious prayer life. There is a strong desire to deepen their awareness of and intimacy with God. However, the efforts often founder on the shoals of good intentions and overcrowded lives. Prayer is something people think about doing after they have taken care of the necessities of life. Once the rest of the daily schedule is accomplished, they will pray. However, the daily schedule is rarely fully accomplished, and prayer is put off until the next day and the next day and the next day.

For those who think that prayer should be spontaneous and a response to the inspiration of the moment, prayer becomes even less frequent. Inspired moments are few in most lives, and if we pray only when we feel like it, we will pray rarely. For some there is resistance to carefully scheduled and disciplined prayer. However, throughout the history of Christianity the great teachers of prayer and spirituality, the people whose lives radiated a deep and transforming faith, were often those for whom prayer had the highest priority in their daily schedule. Many of these people developed and actually wrote rules for living which organized and guided their devotional lives. Some of those rules comprise the subject matter of this book.

Most of us are used to rather tightly scheduled lives. We get up at a regular time in the morning and go to bed at approximately the same time each night. We eat our meals on schedule. We go to work at a certain time and we return to our homes at approximately the same time each day. Some people organize their lives around the television schedule, while others are captive to the timetable of local public transportation. We even go to church according to a rather rigid schedule, a schedule we hope is followed by the Holy Spirit!

But scheduling times for prayer seems almost impossible for most of us, and developing a rhythm or pattern of regularly opening our lives to God in an intensive manner is a frustrating effort. We make our resolutions and set our schedules. All goes well for a few days until something disrupts the process. We try to get back on track, but another exception to the rule occurs. Then one day we cannot concentrate or boredom sets in. Finally, we give up and our resolutions come to nothing.

How have the saints, the great people of prayer who have had such an impact upon the church, done it? How did they organize their lives? In this book we will look at a representative sample of some of the personal rules for life which people composed for themselves, and sometimes for their communities, in an effort to organize their own spiritual lives. At the end of each chapter will be an outline summary for review. Finally, some ideas will be suggested for developing our own personal rules, appropriate for our own life-styles and situations. Most of us cannot live the kind of life many of these folks did. We are not monks or recluses or wandering ascetics. Although many of these people lived extremely busy lives, they had opportunities for prayer that we do not have. Imitating them is not our goal. However, we can learn from them much about how to pray and what place that should have in our normal patterns of living.

We also must keep the idea of a personal rule in perspective. Our goal is not to follow a schedule or a routine of prayer for its own sake. The purpose of a rule is to enable us to live the gospel. It should help deepen our awareness of the divine presence which in turn motivates our actions and determines our values. The development of a personal rule will require much experimentation and revision. Adjustments will be necessary as conditions in our lives change. However, the only way to grow spiritually is to be intentional about it, to make our devotional activity as integral to our lives as eating or sleeping or going to work. So we will look at how people throughout Christian history have done it, and perhaps we will find guidance and inspiration.

A secondary purpose of this book is to introduce the reader to some of the great teachers of prayer in Christian history. We will look at the work of writers from the second, third, fifth, sixth, twelfth, thirteenth, sixteenth, seventeenth and eighteenth centuries as well as that of nine people in the twentieth century. All have something important to say to us.

Finally, I would like to express appreciation to the trustees of Lexington Theological Seminary for granting me a study leave to complete the project and to Dean Clark Gilpin and the community of the Disciples Divinity House of the University of Chicago for marvelous hospitality during the leave. My colleagues on the faculty of Lexington Theological Seminary are a constant source of encouragement.

RULES ON HOW TO PRAY

How do you pray? It seems like such a simple question. Everyone knows how to pray. You bow your head, close your eyes, and tell God what you want. Simple, or so it seems.

Perhaps you have decided to spend thirty minutes a day in prayer. With renewed commitment and enthusiasm you block out that period of time when you think no one will interrupt you. You find a comfortable chair in a quiet place and begin. Bowing your head you begin to pray. You ask God to help relatives who are sick, friends who are facing problems, and people in your church who have various needs. You pray for Sue and George who are considering divorce, for Uncle Jim who is an alcoholic, for the Smiths whose daughter is on drugs. You pray for your minister or priest who is being unfairly criticized by that small faction in the parish that is never happy with anything.

Perhaps you broaden your horizons a little and pray for world peace, for the hungry, for missionaries, for national leaders. With a slight twinge of guilt you pray for yourself. You know you should not be selfish, but you would so much like that promotion or that raise or that job. Maybe you pray that your spouse or your friend will forgive you for sharp words spoken in momentary anger.

You offer all of these prayers with great sincerity

and then look at the clock. Thirty seconds have passed. You still have twenty-nine-and-a-half minutes to pray. You become restless. Perhaps if you just sit in silence some word from God will come to you. That is when distracting thoughts begin to fill your mind: deadlines that must be met, appointments to be kept, responsibilities to be fulfilled, things to be done. You try to push these distractions away, but the more you struggle the more anxious you become. The clock ticks slowly, and if you continue trying to pray through the thirty-minute period, you find yourself frustrated and disappointed that the experience was not peaceful. You had sought a time of calm and it turned out to be stressful, and now you have a headache. If this is prayer, you say to yourself, I must find a better way to develop my faith.

The assumption that everyone knows how to pray is false. Prayer is a great treasure for the religious person, but few have been adequately instructed in it so that it can become a rich experience. How can we learn to pray well?

I would suggest that we look at the instruction of five great teachers of prayer in the Christian tradition, people who wrote simple rules of prayer for us. One was an early church father, Origen; the second was a monk who lived in the declining years of the Roman Empire, John Cassian; two were leaders of the Protestant Reformation in the sixteenth century, Martin Luther and John Calvin; and the fifth is a twentieth century archbishop in the Orthodox Church.

One of the problems with the experience of prayer just described is that it assumed that the purpose of prayer is to get God to do things for us. It saw prayer as a problem solving activity. My hope is that by the end of this book you will see prayer in much broader and deeper ways. These five teachers will present other dimensions of prayer to us, dimensions that if taken seriously can greatly enrich the experience.

ORIGEN

Origen was born around 185 in Alexandria, Egypt, and died around 254. We know little about his early life. He apparently received a good education and supported his mother and other family members by teaching. His father had been martyred by the Romans. Origen was said to have lived a very simple, ascetic life. He took Matthew 19:12 literally and became a "eunuch for the kingdom of God." There is a legend that he wanted to be martyred in a persecution, but his mother prevented this by hiding his clothes.

In time he became the head of a catechetical school in Alexandria, but eventually gave this up and devoted himself to study and writing. He traveled about the Roman Empire, visiting the leading cities and churches. He preached and adjudicated theological disputes. During the persecution of the Emperor Decius around 250, Origen was captured and severely tortured. Although the Romans did not kill him, he died a few years later of broken health, and has been regarded by many as a martyr.

Origen was a Christian philosopher. He believed that the truths of Christianity were universal and had been discovered by pagan thinkers without knowing it. Among his many writings is a fine treatise called *On Prayer* from which we can learn much.

Origen knew some of the questions we have about prayer. For example, why should we pray when God already knows what we need? His answer was that we are free and rational people, responsible for our actions. The evil we do is our own fault. If we pray to be better people, God will send a ministering angel to help us.

When beginning to pray, Origen believed, we should compose our minds properly for prayer. Turning our attention to God and blocking out all other thoughts and interests for a time is profitable, even if nothing more comes of prayer. We are told to "stretch out holy hands" toward God by ridding ourselves of anger. It is important to be calm and orderly in soul and body, standing in awe of God. This preparation must be done before we even begin to offer any prayers to God.

Origen had strong opinions about how *not* to pray. We should not use vain repetitions, we should not ask for little or earthly things, we should not pray with anger or troubled thoughts, we should not pray without purifying ourselves, and we should not pray without the forgiveness of sins. The ultimate goal of prayer is to look beyond earthly things, to see beyond the created order, and arrive at the contemplation of God. Here is a statement on the purpose of prayer that we ought to take seriously. We pray to know God, not to give God orders.

In terms of a rule for prayer, Origen specified that the Christian should pray no less than three times each day: morning (Psalm 5:3), evening (Psalm 141:2), and at midnight (Psalm 119:62). A number of passages from the gospels are cited to indicate how frequently Jesus prayed, as well as examples from other parts of the Bible. If all of these people prayed regularly, why shouldn't we, Origen asked.

At two different points in the treatise, Origen listed those things for which we should pray. He insisted that we pray for the things "that are chiefly and truly great and heavenly." Material and corporeal things, he said, are just a "fleeting and feeble shadow," and can in no way be compared with the "saving and holy gifts of the God of all."

Origen suggested an outline for our prayer:

1. Praise
2. Thanksgiving
   a. for benefits others receive from God
   b. for benefits we receive from God
3. Confession
   a. confession of sins
   b. for healing and deliverance from the habits that bring us to sin
   c. for forgiveness
4. Petitions for great and heavenly things
5. Doxology, praise to God through Christ in the Holy Spirit

We should note that petitions come only after praise, thanksgiving, and confession.

Here is an outline for prayer that we could follow with great profit. It points to the difference between authentic prayer and the example used at the beginning of this chapter. Only after we have praised God, offered our thanksgiving, and confessed our sins, do we begin to petition God. And, Origen warns us, our petitions should be for great and heavenly things, not the fleeting trivialites of life. Finally, we conclude with a doxology, a prayerful song of praise to God.

In a section of the treatise called "Special Directions," Origen presented some curious but useful suggestions for prayer. The proper disposition for prayer, he said, requires withdrawal and preparation. We should cast away all temptation and troubling thoughts and remind ourselves as far as we are able of the majesty whom we approach. We should not approach God "carelessly, sluggishly, and disdainful." We should rid ourselves of any malice we have toward anyone.

The proper posture for prayer, said Origen, is hands outstretched and eyes lifted up. We can sit if we are having trouble with our feet or lie down if we are sick. There are occasions where we may be unable to withdraw from others and must pray as though we were not doing it. Origen did not want us to make a public spectacle of our private prayer. We should kneel when confessing sins and praying for healing and forgiveness.

In discussing the proper place for prayer, Origen said that every place is suitable if one prays well. However, it is highly desirable that we have a special place for prayer in our own house. Ideally, it should not be a place where evil has been done because God flees such places. When praying, we ought to look to the east, "since this is a symbolic expression of the soul's looking for the rising of the true Light."

So Origen expands our definition of prayer. It is not just asking, it is also praising, thanking, and confessing. Its goal is not to gain favors from God, but to look beyond the immediate world to the contemplation of God.

JOHN CASSIAN

Our second teacher of prayer in this chapter is John Cassian, 360–435. He lived at a time when many Christians, unable to stand life in the cities of the declining Roman Empire, fled to the deserts of Egypt and Syria to live as hermits. They wanted to devote themselves to achieving Christian perfection and deepening their relationships with God. They felt that they had to free themselves from the temptations of the culture.

Historically, these people have been called the desert fathers, although there were also women who took up this solitary life. Various collections of stories about these hermits as well as pithy sayings by them were collected, and from these we can learn much. John Cassian was one of the compilers of this material. He joined a monastery in Bethlehem, but soon left and traveled through the desert to interview the hermits, recording what he learned in his *Conferences*.

Two of his conferences were with a desert father named Isaac. Cassian asked Abba Isaac how to maintain unceasing prayer. The conference began with a discussion of the preparations necessary for authentic prayer. The goal was "imperturbable peace and purity of mind" as the context for prayer, but such an achievement, as we know from our own experience, is not easy. We always seem to be faced with those unwanted thoughts and distractions buffeting our minds.

Abba Isaac's advice was that we must prepare for prayer by living virtuously. Without virtue, no one can attain a peaceful mind. The soul must be cleared of sin and passion so that a foundation of simplicity and humility can be built. Proper prayer can be offered only if one is free of worrying about business, of gossip, of anger, of love of money. Whatever we have been thinking about before we pray will come into our minds while we pray. So, before we pray we must become the kind of people we want to be while we are praying. What we do not want to disrupt our prayer, we must keep out of our lives while we are not praying. By clearing the ground, as

Isaac put it, we attain a state of simplicity and innocence which provides a proper context for authentic prayer.

Abba Isaac listed four kinds of prayers:

1. Supplication: prayer for the pardon of sins.
2. Prayers: prayer that vows to serve God with the whole heart.
3. Intercessions: prayers for others.
4. Thanksgiving: prayer offered when the mind recollects what God has done or is doing.

We all need to pray each of these kinds of prayers. However, Abba Isaac also suggested at what points in our spiritual development each was appropriate:

1. Supplication is good for beginners.
2. Prayers are for people who have begun to make some progress toward goodness.
3. Intercessions are for people who are fulfilling vows and see the needs of others.
4. Thanksgiving is for those who are reflecting on the mercy of God and are rapt away into indescribable prayer.

Supplication and prayers focus on ourselves, intercessions focus on others, thanksgiving focuses on God.

In this context, Abba Isaac spoke of our prayer developing to the point that we are "rapt away into that spark-like prayer which no mortal can understand or describe." This is a wordless prayer and appears like the leaping of a flame. When praying we are not even conscious of its content, but simply pour forth prayer to God.

Any of us, regardless of our state of development,

can experience this kind of prayer. However, Isaac suggested beginning with prayer to eradicate sin and acquire virtue before attempting to move on to higher levels of prayer. This loftier state of prayer is formed by charity and the contemplation of God, when the mind is occupied with loving God. In prayer we are facing a great mystery which words fail adequately to describe. Isaac quoted St. Antony, the prototype desert monk, as having said that if a monk understands a prayer being prayed, it is not perfect prayer

Abba Isaac also gave a little commentary on the Lord's Prayer which he described as the pattern of perfect prayer that can carry us to higher states of prayer. Other things which might stimulate such prayer are the verse of a psalm that particularly strikes us, words from a holy person, the death of a friend, or the memory of our own half-heartedness.

What kinds of prayer does God hear? First, Abba Isaac said that we are heard in proportion to how much we believe God looks at us and grants our prayer. In short, we must pray without hesitation or any touch of hopelessness. Second, quoting from Matthew 18:19, Isaac said if two people agree, their prayer will be heard. Third, a prayer prayed in the fullness of faith is heard. Fourth, God hears persevering prayers. Fifth, prayers related to almsgiving, a reformed life, or works of mercy, will be heard. Finally, prayers of agony and suffering are heard. However, if one doubts a prayer will be heard, it will not be. We should avoid hopelessness in prayer.

This conference ended with a few brief admonitions about prayer. When Christ told us to go into our closet and shut the door, this meant, according to Isaac, that we should pray in silence with a concentrated heart and mind. This will keep us from disturbing others and will prevent demons from knowing what we are doing. We should pray often, but briefly.

Cassian was so moved by this conference with Abba Isaac that he asked the desert father to teach him more the next day, so there is a second conference on prayer by Abba Isaac in Cassian's material. This conference opened with a discussion of a serious problem for many religious people, and that is the tendency to attribute human characteristics or anthropomorphic images to God. The highest levels of prayer involve the use of no images. Many of the desert fathers had trouble with this. A Cappadocian deacon named Photinus went to a group of them and explained, "that unmeasurable, incomprehensible, invisible majesty cannot be limited by a human frame or likeness. His nature is incorporeal, uncompounded, simple, and cannot be seen by human eyes nor conceived adequately by a human mind." The more we ponder the mystery of God, the deeper our prayer becomes. In a pure state of prayer, said Isaac, "no effigy of God" will be mingled with one's prayers.

In this conference Cassian asked the Abba how to reach a state of pure prayer. Isaac gave several suggestions. First, one must abandon the contemplation of earthly and material things and seek a state of purity. Only those with the purest sight can look upon the divinity of Jesus.

In withdrawing apart to pray Jesus gave us an example. If we want to address God with a "heart of integrity" we must withdraw from the things in the world that disturb our peace. The mind must be lifted above the material sphere to the realm of the spirit.

Cassian and his friend Germanus remarked, however, that they did not know how to attain the disciplined life that produces the kind of purity of which Abba Isaac spoke. How does one reach the point where one can "cleave to God continually"? What are the first principles or foundations on which one can build such a life? How can one become recollected so that the awareness of God is permanent?

Abba Isaac answered with a "formula for contemplation." It was used by those monks who wanted continual recollection of God, and dated back to the earliest desert fathers. The formula was the first verse of Psalm 70: "Be pleased, O God, to deliver me! O Lord, make haste to help me." This simple verse contains everything needed for the spiritual quest. It calls upon God, it confesses faith, it is a meditation on our frailty and need for God, it expresses confidence in God's answer, and it assures God's support. Isaac said that those who continually call upon God are aware that God is close at hand. The verse is a cure for depression and despair, and those who are making spiritual progress are warned by it that they would have made no progress without God's help.

Isaac described in the conference how he used the verse: when tempted to eat too much, when struggling with lust, when falling asleep while reading the Bible, or when trying to overcome anger, avarice, melancholy or wandering thoughts. It is a prayer that should be prayed in all conditions of life, whether in adversity or prosperity. It should be prayed in our hearts constantly. It teaches us a noble poverty, that ultimately we have nothing but God.

What has Cassian added to our understanding of prayer? Abba Isaac insisted that the moral quality of our lives affects how we pray. Growing in virtue is an important preparation for prayer. He also emphasized that the nature of prayer changes as we grow. We begin with the recognition of our weaknesses, confessing our sins, but we hope to grow to the point that we are "rapt away into indescribable prayer." The life of prayer is not static, and however we design our own personal rule for prayer, we must allow for the changes that growth produces. The highest level of prayer, for Abba Isaac, was nonverbal. It was simply a matter of loving God who is a mystery that transcends the limits of our finite minds.

The next two teachers of prayer mentioned in this chapter were active theologians during the sixteenth century. Their work resulted in the establishment of the Protestant traditions, and their influence is still strong today.

MARTIN LUTHER

Martin Luther is often referred to as "the father of Protestantism." Born in 1483 in northeastern Germany, Luther grew up in a family that rose successfully from peasant poverty to capitalistic prosperity. He was very sensitive religiously and lived in a culture where popular piety saw God as the terrible judge who took delight in casting recalcitrant sinners into hell. Luther wondered if he was good enough to please God and avoid damnation. The religious culture of his time placed heavy emphasis on the importance of good works to assure salvation, and Luther feared he had not done enough. After his university studies he decided to become a monk, hoping that God would then be pleased with him. In time, however, he began to worry about whether he had not kept some rule or displeased God in some other way. It is said that when he went to confession he would confess sins he had not even committed so that if he had left something out he would be covered.

His monastic community recognized Luther as someone who might have a future in academic life and prepared him for teaching. He took a post at a new university in Wittenberg and began to lecture on the Bible. While studying Paul's letter to the Romans he had an insight, an illumination, that changed his life. He was particularly interested in Romans 1:16–17 which states that the gospel is "the power of God for salvation to everyone who has faith, . . . for in it the righteousness of God is revealed, through faith for faith." The phrase that tormented Luther was *justitia Dei,* the righteousness of God. He interpreted that to mean the active justice of God whereby the saints are rewarded and sinners are condemned to everlasting hell. How could he ever be good enough to merit reward, he wondered.

As he pondered the passage, however, he began to notice that he had not put adequate emphasis on the first part, that the gospel is "the power of God for salvation to everyone who has faith." In fact, verse 17 included a quotation from the prophet Habakkuk: "He who through faith is righteous shall live." In short, Luther concluded that our relationship with God is not based on the doing of good works but is based on faith, which Luther defined as trusting in the mercy of God. He came to see the righteousness of God as the faithfulness of God. Our hope for salvation is that God is faithful and fulfills the promises of the gospel.

This gave Luther a whole new outlook on life and Christianity. The churches which followed his leadership became known as Lutheran churches. Their two most dominant characteristics were belief in salvation by faith, not works, and the word of God as the highest authority for the Christian. The Protestant Reformation, as this movement was known, produced many martyrs, ultimately hundreds of new Christian denominations, and major changes in western civilization.

Luther was known as a theologian and reformer. He was also a man of prayer. One of his best known writings on that subject was a little treatise he wrote in 1535 for his barber, Peter Beskendorf, called "A Simple Way to Pray." It provides good guidance for one who wishes to have a serious prayer life but does not know how to begin. The little booklet was immediately popular. Four editions were printed the first year, and ultimately twenty-two editions appeared.

Luther began by saying that when problems began to overwhelm him so that he was distracted from prayer, he would take his Psalter, or book of psalms, and hurry to his room or to the church if a congregation was gathered. He would then say to himself the Ten Commandments, the Apostles' Creed, some psalms, and some words of Christ or Paul, "just as a child might do."

However, he also urged prayer on a regular basis, suggesting that it be the first business of the morning and the last thing one does at night. He warned against putting prayer off until a more convenient time. Other matters will soon dominate the day and prayer will not happen. Breaking the habit of prayer will make us lazy, cool, and listless.

After we have prepared ourselves for prayer by doing the things listed above, we should kneel or stand with hands folded and eyes turned toward heaven and confess to God our unworthiness, yet our desire to pray. Then we should pray the Lord's Prayer.

Luther suggested ways to meditate and expand on the Lord's Prayer. For example, after praying, "Hallowed be thy name," we might add personal prayers that God's name be holy throughout the whole world. He also prayed that people be converted to pure doctrine and holy lives.

To the phrase "Thy kingdom come," Luther would add prayers that God defend the faithful against those who would destroy God's kingdom and use their power for their own ambitions. "Thy will be done on earth as it is in heaven," prompted prayers for the conversion of those who resist God's will and for the abilities needed by the faithful to live the gospel.

"Give us this day our daily bread," led to a prayer for "favorable weather and good harvest," and asked that he might manage his family and property well, teaching them "as a Christian should." "Forgive us our trespasses as we forgive those who trespass against us," is followed by a prayer that God would look not upon our sins, but on the forgiveness of sins which we have in Christ. He also suggested praying for the grace to forgive others.

The sixth petition of the Lord's Prayer, "And lead us not into temptation," called for resistance to the devil and alertness to the word of God. "But deliver us from evil," suggested a prayer that God would help us make our way safely through the wickedness of the world and face death not with fear but with firm faith.

Luther added a note that no one is to pray these prayers using his words. Rather, we should let the Lord's Prayer stir our hearts and guide our personal prayers.

Keeping one's attention focused on prayer and avoiding distractions were very important to Luther. We have not prayed well if we cannot remember what we have said. So, as a good barber keeps his eye on the razor lest the customer be cut, we should give full and undivided attention to prayer.

So, this is how Luther used the Lord's Prayer. He told his barber: "To this day I suckle at the Lord's Prayer like a child, and as an old man eat and drink from it and never get my fill. It is the very best prayer, even better than the Psalter, which is so very dear to me. It is surely evident that a real master composed and taught it."

Luther also suggested praying the Ten Commandments in the same manner. Taking a commandment, he considered its instruction, what God demands by it; then thanksgiving; third a confession; and finally a prayer. For example, the first commandment, "You shall have no other gods before me," reminds us that first, we are expected to trust God in all things. Second, we give thanks for God's infinite compassion and care for us. Third, we confess our sin and ingratitude for having ignored the commandment by various acts of idolatry. Finally, we pray that we may have the grace to obey and seek no other consolation than what we find in God. He would follow this same procedure with each commandment.

He did not propose a rigid approach to prayer, but suggested using the Ten Commandments to stimulate prayer one day, a psalm or chapter from the Bible on another day, and use them "as flint and steel to kindle a flame in the heart."

A final suggestion was to use the Apostles' Creed in the same manner. He used the first three articles of the creed to illustrate the use of the same outline followed with the Ten Commandments. For example, "I believe in God the Father Almighty, maker of heaven and earth," stimulates the thought that we are God's creation without which we would not exist. Second, we give thanks to God that he has created us and the world out of nothing. Third, we confess our lack of gratitude for God's creative work. Fourth, we pray for a faith that trusts God as our creator.

What has Luther added to our understanding of prayer? He made great use of scripture and creed to stimulate our prayer, and gave us a method for meditative prayer.

JOHN CALVIN

John Calvin was born in 1509 in Noyon, France, and developed into a bright young humanist, devoted to the study of the great Greek and Roman classics. Although at one time he had begun preparation for the priesthood, he eventually took up the study of law. His real love, however, was the classics, and he published his first book, a commentary on Seneca, in 1532.

Soon after that, however, he experienced some kind of religious conversion in which he felt that God had made him teachable. He identified with the Protestant cause and, after initial efforts at preaching resulted in imprisonment, he decided to take up the life of a quiet scholar. While living in Basle, he wrote the first edition of *The Institutes of the Christian Religion,* an attempt to summarize Protestant theology. Through many successive editions, this book established Calvin as one of the major theologians of the Reformation.

While passing through Geneva in 1536, he was persuaded to stay there and reform the city, making it a Protestant community. However, his reforms proved controversial and the next year he was expelled from the town. In 1541 he returned to Geneva and devoted the rest of his life to its reform, having firmly established himself there by 1555. While some saw Genevan life as unduly restricted and harsh, others regarded it as an ideal Christian commonwealth. He died in 1564, but his work had a lasting influence throughout the Protestant world.

Calvin's theology was based on two fundamental points: our absolute helplessness to attain salvation on our own merits and God's absolute sovereignty over all things. This led him to a doctrine of predestination, the notion that our salvation is the result of God's election of us. God alone determines who will be saved and who will not.

The Institutes is a long work, usually published in two volumes of some 1500 pages. It is divided into four books. The first is on our knowledge of God, the second on our knowledge of Christ, the third on how we receive the grace of Christ, and the fourth on the church and sacraments. Book Three, Chapter XX, contains a discussion on prayer which Calvin described as "the chief exercise of faith" and the means by which we receive God's benefits on a daily basis.

Calvin believed that prayer is the way people connect themselves with the gifts of God. It is the method by which we unearth the treasures of the gospel. Like Origen, Calvin knew that many felt prayer was unnecessary. If God has elected us, what is the point of praying? Calvin gave six reasons for praying:

1. That we might develop a desire to seek God, turning to God in every need.
2. That our hearts may be free of any desire we would not want to put before God, while at the same time we learn to take all of our wishes to God.
3. That our prayer remind us that all benefits come from God.
4. That in having our prayers answered we may meditate upon the kindness of God.

5. That we receive with great joy what has been
obtained by prayer.
6. That our experience with prayer confirm the
providence of God.

Calvin listed several rules for prayer. First, we must
pray with great reverence. Our hearts must be disposed
in a manner appropriate for conversation with God.
They must be free from "carnal cares and thoughts"
which distract us from the contemplation of God,
although anxiety might motivate us to pray. Calvin knew
that the effort to pray often generated a host of irrele-
vant and distracting thoughts. The only way to solve this
problem is to allow ourselves to be overcome by God's
majesty, to have a sense of awe before the divine.
Likewise, we should not ask in prayer for more than the
gospel promises. God, said Calvin, does not yield to our
willfulness, but bridles our wishes.

Because of our human weaknesses, God gives us the
Holy Spirit to teach us to pray and instruct us in what is
right. As Paul wrote to the Romans, "We do not know
how to pray as we ought, but the Spirit himself inter-
cedes for us with sighs too deep for words" (8:26).

The second rule is, being aware of our own weaknesses and insufficiencies, to pray with burning desire.
The perfunctory praying of set forms of prayer will not
do for Calvin. It is not a matter of appeasing God by
devotions, but rather of ardor and eagerness for God. It
is a zeal for the kingdom of God that motivates us to pray
without ceasing.

A third rule for prayer is that we give up all
thoughts of our own glory and self-assurance and plead
for the forgiveness of sins which is the most important
part of prayer. We must be reconciled to God before we

can have the hope of attaining anything. A pure conscience before God confirms within us the promises of the gospel.

Finally, the fourth rule is that we should pray with the certain hope that our prayers will be answered. Jesus said, "Whatever you ask in prayer, believe that you have received it, and it will be yours" (Mark 11:24). We pray in faith, and it is faith that receives whatever God grants in prayer.

However, Calvin insisted that God will not reject imperfect prayers. No one approaches God with the uprightness that is due. So we seek a twofold pardon: pardon for not recognizing the full extent of our sins and pardon for the sins themselves.

Since it is true that none of us is worthy to stand before God, we have been given Jesus Christ as an advocate, a mediator. It is Christ who protects us from "God's dread majesty." It is his grace that makes it possible for us to be heard by God. So, thankfully, we pray in the name of Jesus.

This section of the *Institutes* includes a discussion of public and private prayer. Calvin reminded us that in Matthew 6 Jesus told us to go into our own room and pray in secret. We should seek a retreat where we can descend into our hearts and "enter deeply within." Prayer is lodged principally in our hearts and needs some element of inner tranquility, free of outward cares. Jesus habitually withdrew to quiet places for prayer.

Calvin believed that in private prayer petition and thanksgiving are basically the same. We give thanks for all the good that God provides for us, and we petition God, thankful that our prayers will be heard. Without God we would have nothing, and realizing that moves us to prayers of thanksgiving for the good we do have in life. This is why, Calvin said, Paul encouraged us to pray without ceasing, to give praise and thanks to God for the promises of the gospel.

Jesus, however, did not avoid praying in the midst of a crowd on occasion, and praying in a Christian assembly, publicly, is appropriate. In fact, Calvin said that those who refuse to pray in the Christian community do not know how to pray privately either. His only warning is that those who pray publicly avoid vain repetition or "a great mass of words." Prayer, both public and private, should come from the depths of the heart. Writing at a time in which the Latin mass had been the norm, he said that public prayer must be in the language of the people. In this connection he noted Paul's discussion of the gift of tongues in 1 Corinthians 14, and discounts the necessity of tongues in private as well as public prayer. In fact, he said that the best prayers are sometimes unspoken. However, on occasion we are moved in prayer to break forth in speech and gesture. Such things as kneeling or uncovering the head are practices by which we express deeper reverence to God.

As Origen, Luther, and others before him had done, Calvin gave an exposition of the Lord's Prayer in this section of the *Institutes*. It is a prayer of six petitions. Three are prayers devoted to the glory of God: that God's name be hallowed, that God's kingdom come, that God's will be done. Three express care for ourselves: daily bread, the forgiveness of sins, avoidance of temptation. This is a perfect prayer, Calvin believed. It sets forth what is worthy of asking of God and what God will willingly grant.

Although we should pray without ceasing, human weakness dictates that we should set apart certain times for prayer each day. For Calvin, the best times are:

1. When we awake in the morning.
2. Before we begin daily work.
3. When we sit down for a meal.
4. When we have eaten.
5. When we go to bed.

Praying at these hours should not be seen as paying a debt to God, but as "a tutelage for our weakness." We should also pray when we or others are facing adversity, or when we or others rejoice in prosperity.

Finally, Calvin concluded this section of the *Institutes* by advising patient perseverance in prayer. It is important to wait for God, knowing that God is always present to us. Our prayers are never in vain.

It is interesting that one with so high a view of God's sovereignty that the logical conclusion is predestination should take prayer so seriously. Calvin implied what many of the saints have said, that the real purpose of prayer is to deepen our intimacy with God, to open our lives to the divine. He could not ignore the fact that scripture teaches us to pray, and in the Lord's Prayer we have the perfect model. God may not need our prayers, but our human weakness needs the growth and insight that prayer produces.

ANTHONY BLOOM

This section must conclude with a writer from our own century. Anthony Bloom's little book, *Beginning to Pray,* has remained in print for over twenty years and is a fine introduction to prayer. His biography is fascinating. He was born in Switzerland in 1914, the son of a Russian diplomat. Soon afterwards the family moved to

Persia, where his father served. After the Russian Revolution the family settled in Paris. Bloom became a physician, serving as a surgeon in a Paris hospital during World War II and aiding the Resistance. He took monastic vows secretly and was ordained in 1948. Eventually he became a bishop, then archbishop, and, finally, Metropolitan of the Russian Orthodox Church, responsibile for Orthodoxy in Great Britain and Ireland. He brings to a discussion of prayer a scientific background and the traditions of eastern Christianity.

For Bloom, there are certain realities we must face before we pray. The first is to recognize our own poverty. We have nothing that we can keep forever. We exist because we have been willed into existence. However, everything we possess is a sign of the love of God. Still, Bloom says that we cannot live a life of prayer unless we are free from a sense of possession. We must offer both hands to God and have a heart that is absolutely open.

In focusing our prayer, we must avoid using any images of God. Imprisoning God in our own concepts or images makes the encounter more difficult. We must stand before God with open minds. The first place to look for God is within ourselves, where the kingdom of God is. Bloom uses a famous quote from John Chrysostom, a bishop in the fourth and fifth centuries: "Find the door of your heart, and you will discover it is the door of the kingdom of God." It is important not to seek a God who is far off, but the God who is within us.

Now, what do we do when the actually pray? First, says Bloom, we must choose a prayer. The right words are important in establishing a relationship with someone. We should find words that are worthy of us and worthy of God.

He suggests three kinds of prayer. First, spontaneous prayers, when we are vividly aware of God or when we are in such distress that we know God is our only help. However, we cannot sustain spontaneous prayer throughout our lives. So Bloom suggests moving on to existing prayers, the phraseology of which may express what we want to pray. His specific example is the psalms in the Old Testament. He recommends marking passages which go deep into our hearts and express our own experience. If we learn such passages by heart, they will come into our minds when we need them as a gift from God. Finally, Bloom suggests the Jesus Prayer, a major Orthodox form of devotion. It is a simple, but complete prayer: "Lord Jesus Christ, son of God, have mercy on me a sinner." It is a profession of faith and a recognition of our own situation.

For Bloom, prayer is an encounter and a relationship that cannot be forced. An encounter with God is always a moment of judgment. However, as long as we are real, truly ourselves, God can be present with us. A false self cannot be approached by God.

SUMMARY

What rules for prayer can we draw from these five people? They can be summarzied as follows:

Origen

1. Prayer begins with the proper mental preparation.
2. We should pray three times a day.
3. Major elements in prayer:
   a. Praise

    b. Thanksgiving
    c. Confession
    d. Petition
    e. Doxology.

John Cassian and Abba Isaac

1. The goal of prayer is "imperturbable peace and purity of mind."
2. Prepare for prayer by living virtuously.
3. Four kinds of prayer:
    a. Supplication—prayer for pardon.
    b. Prayers—vows to serve God with the whole heart.
    c. Intercessions—prayer for others.
    d. Thanksgiving—for all God has done and is doing.
4. Prayers God hears:
    a. Prayers are heard in proportion to how much we believe God hears us.
    b. When two people agree.
    c. Prayers prayed in the fulness of faith.
    d. Persevering prayers.
    e. Prayers of agony and suffering.
5. Additional rules:
    a. Pray silently.
    b. Pray briefly but often.
    c. Pray using no images of God.
6. How to reach a pure state of prayer:
    a. Abandon the contemplation of earthly and material things.
    b. Address God with a heart of integrity.
    c. Use Psalm 70:1.

Martin Luther

1. In praying, use the Ten Commandments, the creed, the psalms, and words of Christ or Paul.
2. Pray morning and evening.
3. Meditate carefully on the phrases of the Our Father.
4. Meditate on the Ten Commandments:
   a. What does the commandment say?
   b. Give thanks for God's compassion.
   c. Confess that we have violated the commandment.
   d. Pray for the grace to obey it.

John Calvin

1. Reasons to pray:
   a. That we might develop a desire for God.
   b. That our hearts may be free of anything we would not want to put before God.
   c. That prayer remind us of God's benefits to us.
   d. That when our prayers are answered we might meditate on the kindness of God.
   e. That we receive with joy what has come from our prayer.
   f. That our experience with prayer may confirm the providence of God.
2. Ways to pray:
   a. Pray with great reverence.
   b. Pray with burning desire.
   c. Pray for the forgiveness of sins.
   d. Pray with the hope that prayer will be answered.
3. Times for prayer:
   a. When we awake in the morning.

    b. Before beginning daily work.
    c. Before meals.
    d. At the end of a meal.
    e. When we go to bed.

Anthony Bloom

Preparation for prayer:
1. Realize our poverty, that we keep nothing forever.
2. Everything we have is a sign of the love of God.
3. We have been willed into existence by God.
4. Avoid images of God.
5. Understand that God is to be found within us.

What to pray:
1. Spontaneous prayers.
2. Biblical prayers and those others have composed, the phraseology of which expresses what we want to pray.
3. The Jesus Prayer in the Orthodox tradition.

What have we learned from these five teachers of prayer? We have seen that prayer is far more than closing our eyes and asking God to do things for us. Consider these summary points:

1. Good prayer requires preparation. We must learn to calm ourselves and achieve some level of stillness and peace before we pray.
2. In prayer we are confronting mystery. God far transcends any mental images we may have, and we must recognize that they are a hindrance in prayer.
3. There are many other kinds of prayer than just

petition. Good prayer includes praise, adoration, thanksgiving, and confession. The emphasis should be on God, not ourselves.

4. The most important purpose of prayer is the contemplation of God, deepening our intimacy with the divine.

2

RULES FOR MAINTAINING A REGULAR PRAYER LIFE

Let us return for a moment to the example of the unfortunate experience with prayer described in the beginning of the previous chapter. Suppose you follow some of the advice and instruction from our five teachers in chapter 1. You begin to see prayer as a deeper matter than just asking God to give you things. You do begin to praise and offer thanksgiving and confess your weaknesses. You use that thirty-minute period to meditate on scripture or the creed. You ponder quietly the mystery of God and begin to develop a sense of being overwhelmed by mystery.

All goes well for several weeks and you can begin to sense some subtle changes in yourself. Then your schedule is disrupted. Out of town visitors come for a few days. A member of the family gets sick and needs attention. An upheaval at work produces anxiety and you have trouble relaxing and settling down. The church asks you to take on some responsibility that consumes all of your spare time. Suddenly that thirty minutes that you blocked out for prayer in your schedule has vanished. How do you find it again?

There could be another problem, however. Some people think that prayer should be spontaneous, that it should not be tied to a schedule, that it is hypocritical to pray when they do not feel like it. When they are busy they never feel like praying, so prayer becomes very infrequent if it is done at all.

As we have noted, whether we want them to be or not, many parts of our lives are rather rigidly scheduled. All of this scheduling reveals that we will find time for the things we really want to do.

In this chapter we will look at rules for prayer which attempt to integrate prayer into the schedule of daily living. Some may appear to be too rigid and may prescribe more than anyone living a normal life in the world could possibly do. However, the principle of scheduling prayer as we would the other elements of our lives is worth examination.

Six rules will be examined in this chapter: a second century church manual called *The Didache*; the most famous monastic rule in western civilization, the *Rule* of St. Benedict; a personal prayerbook, the *Private Devotions* of Lancelot Andrewes; *A Serious Call to a Devout and Holy Life* by William Law; a little prayer book and *Scheme for Self-Examination* by John Wesley; and some suggestions from Orthodox Archbishop Anthony Bloom's *Beginning to Pray.*

THE DIDACHE

The Didache, or as it is sometimes known, *The Teaching of the Twelve Apostles,* has fascinated church historians for what it reveals to us about life in the early church. Long unknown, this document was discovered in 1873. It was probably written in the mid-second century as a little rule for new converts. Among other things, it describes early Christian worship and eucharistic celebration. It also reveals an order of ministry consisting of bishops and deacons, as well as wandering prophets about whom Christians should be suspicious if they stay around more than three days.

The *Didache* contains a number of quotations from the Bible that describe how we should live, what we should and should not do. It encourages us to love God and neighbor, to turn the other cheek, to give to those who beg from us, and to avoid magic, sorcery, abortion, irritability, lust, divination, grumbling, and presumptuousness. Children should be taught to revere God.

Anticipating a practice that John Wesley encouraged, the *Didache* instructs us to confess our sins at church meetings and pray with a good conscience. As far as scheduling is concerned, the *Didache* advised fasting on Mondays and Thursdays because the hypocrites fast on Wednesdays and Fridays. The Lord's Prayer should be prayed three times a day.

This is a brief, simple little rule. It depicts a life-style of prayer, fasting, and virtue. Praying the Lord's Prayer three times a day should not strain anyone, but it begins to instill the notion of disciplined prayer within us.

As the history of Christianity unfolded there developed the practice of praying at stated hours of the day. The book of Acts mentions Peter praying on the housetop at the sixth hour of the day (10:9), and tells of Peter and John going to the temple "at the hour of prayer, the ninth hour" (3:1). Acts also reveals to us that Cornelius "was keeping the ninth hour of prayer" (10:30). These were Jewish hours of prayer that Christians continued to observe.

In ancient times it was assumed that the first hour of the day was at sunrise, or approximately 6:00 A.M.

This means that the sixth hour would be noon, the ninth hour would be 3:00 P.M.

Some Christians began to pray at intervals observing events relating to the death of Christ. They would pray at the third hour, or 9:00 A.M., in observance of the time Jesus was crucified (Mark 15:25); the sixth hour, noon, when darkness covered the land (Mark 15:33); and the ninth hour, 3:00 P.M., the time when Jesus died (Mark 15:34). In some monasteries there was also a time of prayer at the first hour, 6:00 A.M.

Later there were added an early morning period of prayer called lauds, the Latin word for praise, and an evening period called vespers, from the Latin for evening. Eventually, there appeared a period of night prayers, called either vigils or matins, and a time of prayer at the end of the day called compline, to complete the day.

In the Middle Ages, pious laypeople who wanted to observe these times of prayer owned Books of Hours which contained the Old Testament psalms arranged appropriately for each period of prayer. These books, copied by hand, are appreciated today for their artistic value.

As Christian monasticism developed, the community life revolved around prayer services at these times of the day. The times were called the canonical hours and the services were called Divine Offices. They involved praying the psalms from the Old Testament. Hymns, scripture readings, and responses filled out the services. The service book for these offices today is called the breviary. In recent years, the breviary has been revised to include only morning, midday, and evening prayer. An additional office of readings may be used at any time. The principle of regular prayer at various intervals throughout the day, however, has been maintained.

BENEDICT

One of the major examples of periodic daily prayer has been the Christian monastic tradition. The hermit life of the desert fathers and mothers eventually evolved into a communal form where people would live and pray together. There were a number of early rules written to govern the monastic life, but the most important and influential was the *Rule* of St. Benedict of Nursia.

Benedict of Nursia has been one of the major influences on western civilization. His design of the monastic life flourished in the Middle Ages and provided an organizing principle for community living that gave stability to a precarious culture.

He was born around 480, after the Roman Empire in the west had been overrun by so-called barbarians. The last Roman emperor had been deposed just a few years earlier. In this context, young Benedict went to Rome for his education, but became discouraged at the immorality of Roman society. Moving to a cave at Subiaco, some thirty miles east of Rome, he took up the life of a hermit and sought to deepen his religious life. In time, he attracted the attention of others who wanted to live a similar life, and they asked him to be their abba, or abbot. He organized them into groups of twelve. However, some of the local clergy became jealous of his fame as a holy man, and eventually he left to establish a monastery at Monte Cassino, about halfway between Rome and Naples. There he developed his famous *Rule* for the monastery. Eventually this became the most widely used monastic rule in Europe and, indeed, is followed in many monasteries today. Benedict died around 547, but the influence of his *Rule* is still very much with us. Although it has to be adapted to the conditions of modern life, the basic principles of it are followed in many modern monastic communities.

Benedict defined a monastery as "a school for the Lord's service." After a trial period of one year during which the *Rule* would be read to the candidate several times, a monk would take lifetime vows of stability, obedience, and fidelity to the monastic life. Stability meant that the monk would stay is his monastery until death. Obedience was obedience to the superiors, especially the abbot who was the head of the community, and fidelity to the monastic life included such things as poverty and celibacy. One of the reasons for the success of the *Rule* was its moderation. Benedict wanted a rule that contained "nothing harsh, nothing burdensome," a rule that the average person could follow and that did not require heroic self-denial. All things, said Benedict, should be done in moderation. Still, many of us would find the life difficult at best.

The life of the community was to be a cycle of prayer, reading, and manual labor. Believing that idleness is the enemy of the soul, Benedict prescribed a tightly scheduled life in which there was virtually no free time. A typical schedule for prayer in a Benedictine monastery in the Middle Ages might have looked like this:

2:00 A.M.	Vigils or Matins
5:00 A.M.	Lauds
6:00 A.M.	Prime (first hour)
9:00 A.M.	Terce (third hour)
Noon	Sext (sixth hour)
3:00 P.M.	None (ninth hour)
5:00 P.M.	Vespers
7:00 P.M.	Compline

These were services at which the psalms were prayed. *Lectio divina*, devotional reading, was part of the monk's routine, and manual labor, which provided the means of support for the community, filled out the daily schedule.

What value does a rule for a monastic community have for us? There are a number of principles for ordering our lives in this rule that could prove useful to us to anyone. Benedict insisted on certain priorities. For example, he believed that the love of Christ should come before anything else.

An important concept in the *Rule* that may benefit us is the notion of the rhythm of the life, keeping a balance between work and prayer. It is probably not practical for most of us to pray seven times a day, but the notion of including regular prayer as part of our normal daily routine is important. Periodically we must drop what we are doing and refocus our attention on God. Related to this is the idea of using the psalms as the basis for our prayer life.

The *Rule* prescribes particular psalms for certain times of the day. For example, at the office of vigils in the middle of the night, the monks were to pray Psalm 3, "I lie down and sleep; I wake again, for the Lord sustains me." The *Rule* states that a minimum of twelve psalms must be prayed at vigils. The office of lauds, which emphasizes the praise of God, begins with Psalm 67: "Let all the peoples praise you, O God, let all the peoples praise you," and concludes with Psalms 148 through 150: "Let everything that breathes praise the Lord."

The offices of prime, terce, sext, and none, are brief times of prayer at which only three psalms are prayed at each service. These services include parts of

Psalm 119, the longest one in the Psalter. It is composed of twenty-two sections, and each is treated as one psalm.

Vespers includes four psalms, beginning always with Psalm 110: "The Lord is at your right hand," and ending with Psalm 147: "It is good to sing praises to our God." The last service of the day, usually done right before the monks go to bed, always uses Psalms 4: "In peace I will both lie down and sleep"; 134: "Who stand by night in the house of the Lord;" and 91: "You will not fear the terrors of the night."

These services also included hymns, scripture readings, and other prayers. They were an attempt to sanctify the time, periodically halting the daily activity and returning one's attention to God's presence.

The use of the psalms as a basis of prayer is a practice that should be seriously considered. It relieves us of the burden of setting an agenda for prayer. We simply pray the prayers God has given us in scripture. We will find that almost everything we would ever want to include in our prayer is to be found somewhere in the Psalter. Some of the psalms lend themselves very easily to prayer. Others are full of vengeance and anger and call for terrible things to happen to the enemy. We can internalize those psalms and pray them against those interior enemies that disrupt our personalities, such as prejudice, anger, envy, pride, selfishness, and other unfortunate qualities. Those are the enemies we want God to destroy.

At the end of the instruction on the Divine Office, Benedict gave advice that we find in so many of the writings of the saints. Prayer, he said, should be brief and pure unless the grace of God inspires us to pray longer. When the community prays together, however, it should always be brief. God is more concerned, he believed, with the purity of our hearts than the length of our prayers.

You will probably never live in a monastery, but you may find some way to regularize your prayer and you may find praying the psalms a deepening devotional practice.

LANCELOT ANDREWES

A third person who had some ideas about maintaining a prayer life was a seventeenth century Anglican bishop named Lancelot Andrewes. Andrewes was a person of major importance in the history of the Church of England. He was born in 1555, and his life spanned at least part of the reigns of Mary, Elizabeth, James I, and Charles I. He was a contemporary of Shakespeare.

His birthplace was London in the parish of All Hallows, Barking. One of his early teachers recognized his intellectual ability and encouraged his parents to provide a good education for him rather than apprentice him to a trade. Eventually, he enrolled at Pembroke College, Cambridge.

Andrewes was a quiet sort and never joined in the usual sports or amusements of students. His main forms of recreation were walking and observing nature. He loved study, an activity that would dominate his life, and was especially proficient in languages. He was said to have known Latin, Greek, Hebrew, Chaldee, Syriac, Arabic, and fifteen modern languages. His knowledge was broad. He was well acquainted with the Greek and Latin classics, the church fathers, the medieval theologians and was also known for his historical scholarship.

His sermons are rich in references to all these fields and their various authors. He was probably best known as a preacher of remarkable ability. In fact, it was said that on the night before his execution, Charles I recommended Andrewes' sermons to Princess Elizabeth.

He served as chaplain to Queen Elizabeth and to the Archbishop of Canterbury, John Whitgift. During the reign of James I he was appointed to three successive bishoprics: Chichester, Ely, and Winchester. Andrewes was one of the translators of the King James Version of the Bible published in 1611 and chaired the committee that translated Genesis through 2 Kings.

During his lifetime, it was his preaching that attracted the most attention. He preached frequently in court, and spoke as one who had experience of what he preached. This would reflect the fact, reported by his contemporaries, that he spent five hours a day in prayer.

It is his prayer life in which we are most interested here. He worked out for himself a personal daily liturgy which, after his death, was published under the title, *Private Devotions.* Not intended for public consumption, the book reflects the faith, piety, and spirituality of Andrewes. The *Private Devotions* became the most widely read and popular work of Anglican devotional literature.

The *Private Devotions* or *Preces Privatae,* the Latin title, reveals much about Andrewes' prayer life and, by implication, his personal faith. It was a personal prayer book, designed for a week, that guided his meditations and prayers in such a way that the whole range of prayer and religious experience would be touched. The prayers and meditations were written in the three languages of the cross: Greek, Latin, and Hebrew, reflecting his personal love of languages. As the writer of one study has stated, the book is a "spiritual commonplace" in that most of the material is borrowed. It is full of biblical quotations, material from the church fathers, phrases from pagan writers, and liturgical material from Greek, Latin, and Jewish sources. The whole work reflected his astonishingly broad learning.

The first full edition of the *Private Devotions* appeared in the original languages in 1675. However, between 1648 and 1903 twenty English editions in various forms were published. The most famous translation was that done by John Henry Newman in 1840 as one of his *Tracts for the Times.* A later translation was published in 1903 by F. E. Brightman. This annotated version is important for scholars and for those interested in the sources of his scriptural and liturgical material. The *Private Devotions* could serve as a good model if you wish to develop your own personal prayer book for use in daily prayer.

There were various editions of the *Private Devotions* in existence when Andrewes died. All were written by hand and some had been given to friends. Today there are many versions and translations available. This chapter will be based on the translation of John Henry Newman, first published in 1840 during his involvement in the Oxford movement. It is somewhat abbreviated, but contains the essence of Andrewes' approach.

There are basically three major sections to the *Private Devotions:* a liturgy for morning prayer and for evening prayer, as well as prayers for each day of the week. These are preceded by an introductory section and followed by "Additional Exercises."

The introductory section is simply a collection of Bible verses about prayer, organized under three headings. Under "Times of Prayer," for example, Andrewes listed such things as Luke 18:1: "They ought always to pray and not lose heart"; 1 Thessalonians 5:17: "Pray constantly"; and Psalm 55:17: "Evening and morning and at noon I utter my complaint and moan and he will hear my voice." He also cited Psalm 119:164: "Seven times a day I praise thee for thy righteous ordinances," and listed those times with scriptural references:

1. In the morning before daybreak. Mark 1:35
2. Morning watch. Psalms 63:6 and 130:6
3. The third hour. (9:00 A.M.) Acts 2:15
4. The sixth hour. (noon) Acts 10:9
5. The ninth hour. (3:00 P.M.) Acts 3:1
6. Eventide. Genesis 24:63
7. Night. Psalm 143:1

Andrewes also added a notation for prayer at midnight, Psalm 119:62.

Second, he listed references in the Bible on the places of prayer. This listing included such things as in a congregation, Psalm 111:1; in one's room or closet, Matthew 6:6; in an upper room, Acts 1:13-14; in the temple, Acts 3:1; in a desert place, Mark 1:35; and in every place, 1 Timothy 2:8.

Finally, Andrewes collected verses on the "Circumstances of Prayer." These included kneeling, Luke 22:41; smiting the breast, Luke 18:13; trembling, Acts 16:29; groaning, Isaiah 59:11; and the raising of the eyes and hands, Psalms 25:15 and 143:6. Andrewes must have reviewed these verses from time to time to remind himself of the physical and outward dimensions of prayer. Specific examples of his prayers will be found in chapter 7.

WILLIAM LAW

A fourth person who can instruct us on maintaining a personal prayer life was William Law of the eighteenth century. He was truly a pious man in the best sense of that word.

Law was born in 1686 at King's Cliffe, Northampton, in England. He enrolled in Emmanuel College at Cambridge with the intention of entering the ministry. Completing his B.A. degree in 1708, he was ordained three years later, receiving in the same year a fellowship to Emmanuel College which made possible the earning of an M.A. degree. His major interests in college were the classics and philosophy, and he developed some ability in Hebrew and French. One of the most important decisions in his life was his refusal to take an oath of allegiance to King George I, rejecting the claim of the House of Hanover to the English throne. Consequently, as a Non-juror he lost his fellowship at Cambridge and the right to function as a priest in the Church of England. After at least fifteen years as a private tutor and chaplain and several years in London, he returned to King's Cliffe permanently.

Now he devoted himself to a rigorous spiritual life as well as works of charity and mercy. He founded a school for orphan girls and a school for boys, gave food and clothing to the poor, and established two almshouses. His daily routine was carefully scheduled. He arose each day at 5:00 A.M. to pray, and after breakfast spent time in study until about 9:00 A.M. Family devotions were followed by more time for study. After a midday meal and devotions with friends, he studied until tea. Then came prayer and Bible reading with the servants. Otherwise, he spent time on his many charitable activities, including distributing milk to the poor from his own cows. Death came in 1761, the result of a kidney disease.

His personal devout life impressed many, but more important for posterity were his writings which ran to nine volumes. Among these are *The Spirit of Love, The Spirit of Prayer, The Way to Divine Knowledge,* and the one in which we are interested, *A Serious Call to a Devout and Holy Life,* written in 1729. In the book, Law complained about people who did not take religion seriously, and created a cast of characters illustrating different kinds of people and their excuses. However, the major part of *A Serious Call* is devoted to a rule for prayer. Law prescribed five times of prayer throughout the day, as well as a topic for each, so that the day is sanctified by regularly opening oneself to God. They were:

Morning prayer	Praise and thanksgiving
9:00 A.M.	Humility
Noon	Universal love and intercession
3:00 P.M.	Conforming to God's will
Evening prayer	Self-examination and confession

"Prayer," he wrote, "is the nearest approach to God and the highest enjoyment of Him that we are capable of in this life. It is the noblest exercise of the soul, the most exalted use of our best faculties, and the highest imitation of the blessed inhabitants of Heaven."

In his discussion of morning prayer, he assumed that the healthy Christian was up early and alert, "not a slave to drowsiness." We should not offer God idle, slothful prayers, but should approach prayer alertly and energetically. Law recommended using prepared forms of prayer in the beginning, but if the inspiration of devotion should move us, we should leave them behind and become more spontaneous. On occasion we may move beyond the use of words in prayer.

The first thing Law recommended we do is use a period of silence to recollect ourselves and become aware that we are in the presence of God. In beginning our prayers we should use words that express the highest attributes of God, the greatness, providence and presence of God. Law's prayers were eloquent, but he believed that this disposed the mind to be aware of the nature of God.

Law prescribed praise and thanksgiving as the subject matter for morning prayer. We should thank God for the new day, a new creation, and should offer our bodies and souls, all that we have, to the service and glory of God. Every new day should be seen as a resurrection from death. Other prayers related to our individual lives could be offered, depending on what Law called the disposition of our states and the disposition of our hearts. The former referred to our external condition: health, troubles, disappointments, relationships with others. The latter referred to the temper of our hearts: joy, peace, anxiety, discontent, resentments, envy and other attitudes. In a little excursus in chapter 15, Law encouraged beginning prayer with a psalm from the Old Testament. "This is so right, is so beneficial to devotion, has so much effect upon our hearts, that it may be insisted upon as a common rule for all persons," he said. However, he did not just prescribe reading a psalm; he insisted that we sing or chant it. This will disperse our dullness of heart, purify the soul from little passions, and carry our hearts to heaven, he believed. We should sing imagining ourselves among the choirs of heaven.

The second period of prayer should be at 9:00 A.M.

or the third hour of the morning. By this time the good Christian would have been at business for several hours and needed to return attention to God. Law's recommendation was that the topic for this period of prayer be humility. No one, said Law, is in greater danger of pride than the one who has made some progress in the pious life. Doing good leaves us open to vanity and self-satisfaction. Therefore, renewing our humility is important. Humility is not having a lower opinion of ourselves than we really deserve. It is a matter of being honestly aware of our weaknesses and our sins. Many of us carry some hidden guilt with which we have never come to terms. If we are honest with ourselves on those matters, we will be authentically humble people. However, humility must be learned, and the dangerous temptation is to believe that one is humble enough. True humility is contrary to the values of the world, so it must be a continual subject of prayer if we would seek such a grace.

Prayer at the sixth hour, or noon, is the third time of prayer during the day. The suggested theme for this time is universal love and intercession. Law defined intercession as "praying to God and interceding with Him for our fellow creatures." He insisted that "there is no principle of the heart that is more acceptable to God than a universal fervent love," for all people. Nothing makes us more like God than to wish and pray for the happiness of all people. Love unites us to God when it is as universal as the love God has for all people. Most of us, as a practical matter, are able to help only a few people. However, if we have a deep love in our hearts for those we are unable to help, God will regard us as having done good to all. But there is another, more important benefit, for intercessory prayer for others. As we offer to God our prayers for others we become more generous and selfish passions begin to die. Law believed that nothing makes us love another person so much as praying for that individual. He did recommend that intercessions be specific, that they relate to the particular circumstances of people we know. That means that our intercessory prayers will change as the needs of those we know change.

Prayer at 3:00 P.M., or the ninth hour, was to have as its subject conformity to the will of God. Virtue, said Law, is a matter of conforming to God's will. Vice is declining to conform to that will. However, resigning ourselves to God's will involves a thankful acceptance of all that comes from God. Theologically, this section of the book reflected Law's belief that our state in life is the result of the eternal purpose and providence of God. Nothing, he believed, happened by chance, but by the infinite wisdom of God.

Finally, the last period of prayer for the day was at 6:00 P.M. As we come to the end of the day the appropriate devotion is self-examination and confession. Once again, Law urged that we be specific. Confession has little benefit unless it involves the specific sins of a particular day. If we pray the same prayer of confession that we prayed yesterday, there is no repentance of the sins of today. Law felt that it was important not to end the day with any sins unrepented.

The method of confession depends upon the particular nature of each individual. Most people have some tendencies that are stronger than others, some sins that are more tempting than others. These should be examined very closely and not simply included in a more general confession. Some people are hot-tempered, some much given to vanity, some inclined to lying. Whatever our biggest problem might be, that part of our character should be looked at carefully in offering our confession to God. Finally, Law suggests that as we go to bed each night we remember that if we see the light of another day it will be because of the mercy of God. We should regard each day as our last and resign ourselves into the hands of God.

Five times a day would be a heavy burden for many, but the principle here is sanctifying the time, regularly turning our attention back to God and opening ourselves to the presence of God. Also useful is the idea of having a different emphasis for each time of prayer. However we do it, turning our attention to God periodically throughout the day is a great principle of devotion.

JOHN WESLEY

Our fourth teacher on how to maintain a serious devotional life is John Wesley. He began a movement for spiritual renewal in eighteenth century England that has continued to this day. Out of the work of John and his brother Charles developed the Methodist churches, one of the largest groups of Protestant Christians in the world. A descendant of two generations of clergy, John was born in Epworth in 1703. Growing up in the rectory, young John learned the importance of discipline, prayer, Bible study, morality, and simple living. He would forever be opposed to extravagance and ostentatiousness. His father emphasized High Church principles, inward religion, and the great mystics. His mother, believing John to be destined for greatness, promoted his spiritual development by regular instruction.

Wesley entered Oxford University in 1720, and in 1726 was named a fellow at Lincoln College, Oxford. This gave him the privilege of preaching without a parish, a development that would be crucial to his future ministry, although at the time he had no idea what was ahead for his life. It would also provide him with financial security as long as he remained unmarried.

At Oxford Wesley became a student of some of the great writers of spiritual classics: Jeremy Taylor, Thomas a Kempis, William Law. In fact, it was the study of Law's *Christian Perfection* and *A Serious Call to a Devout and Holy Life* that produced a major conversion, a realization of the need to devote himself totally to God. He was ordained a priest in the Church of England in 1728.

After serving briefly as his father's assistant, Wesley returned to Oxford to teach and discovered that his brother Charles had organized a small group for Bible study, discipline, and frequent attendance at the eucharist. The group developed an interest in early Christianity, particularly the desert father tradition. The group had its detractors who called it names such as the Holy Club, but Methodist was the title that stuck. John joined the group and began the study of patristic literature of both the east and the west where he encountered the notion of the perfection of the Christian life.

Membership in the Holy Club also marked the beginning of a life-style of asceticism and service. He visited prisons and assisted the poor and the sick. For Wesley there was no such thing as a solitary Christian. Fellowship and service to others and the community were vital to living the gospel. He learned to live on very little and began to fast on Wednesdays and Fridays in keeping with what he believed to be the practice of the ancient church. In all of this his goal was inward holiness.

The Holy Club also emphasized the importance of liturgy, and members took communion frequently. One of his ideas that never became popular among Methodists was that of regular and frequent observance of the lord's supper. The chief means of grace, Wesley said, were prayer, Bible study, and the lord's supper. He even published a sermon on *The Duty of Constant Communion,* and in a letter to Methodists in America, taken there by Thomas Coke, he advised administering the lord's supper every Sunday.

In 1733, while teaching at Oxford, Wesley published his first work, *A Collection of Forms of Prayer for Every Day in the Week.* Intended for the use of his students, the book had gone through nine editions by 1755, and Wesley included it in the collected edition of his works in 1772. Later he published *A Collection of Prayers for Families* and *Devotions for Every Day in the Week and the Great Festivals.* Selections from these were published in 1951, edited by Frederick C. Gill, a British Methodist.

In the preface to the first collection, Wesley stated his purpose. He wanted to have forms of prayer for each day of the week which would include deprecation, petition, thanksgiving, and intercession. Wesley's own practice was to spend an hour in prayer in the morning and another hour in the evening, so this collection includes prayers for both periods. He also wanted prayers for use in particular seasons and festivals of the Christian year, as well as prayers that would include petitions for "the whole scheme of our Christian duty." Our Christian duty, he said, included five items: the renunciation of self, devoting ourselves to God, self-denial, mortification to the point that we desire nothing but God, and the reality of Christ living in us. Examples of his prayers will be found in chapter 7.

Other features of Wesley's personal rule are seen in

A Scheme for Self-Examination used by the Oxford Holy
Club or the first Methodists, as the group was sometimes
called. Members of the group confessed to each other
and shared the state of their souls. They were to pray
brief ejaculatory prayers on the hour, they were to pray
collects (brief, one-sentence prayers) at 9:00 A.M., noon,
and 3:00 P.M., they were to meditate at 6:00 P.M. All of
this in addition to the basic morning and evening periods of prayer.

The outline of self-examination included the following questions:

—Has anything been done without knowing it was
  the will of God?
—Has prayer been offered with fervor? Was prayer
  offered entering and leaving church, morning and
  evening in private?
—Have one to three hours of prayer been offered?
—Have prayers been offered for humility, faith, hope
  and love?
—Have the three collects been offered each day as
  well as a meditation?
—Has there been zeal for doing good?
—Has at least an hour a day been spent talking to
  another person?
—Has religion been explained to a stranger?
—Have others been persuaded to attend church ser-
  vices?
—Has another been spoken to unkindly?
—Has a neighbor been rejoiced or grieved with over
  virtues and pleasures or pain and sin?

These are examples of questions one would ask publicly
or privately in self-examination. Wesley was nothing if

not methodical in his spirituality. His prayer life was carefully organized, scheduled, and worked out theologically. Perhaps some would find him too rigid, but he believed that serious discipline was essential to spiritual growth. However, the maintenance of such austerity was not the goal of life. All of these practices had as their aim joy and peace in faith. Wesley believed that holiness was happiness. The deepest joy in life was to be found in the cultivation of perfection and intimacy with God.

Soon after the death of his father, John and a few other members of the group, under the patronage of the Society for the Propagation of the Gospel, decided to go to Georgia as missionaries to the Indians and, ultimately, to the colonists there. The mission was a failure for a variety of reasons, including a disastrous love affair, and Wesley returned to England.

However, there were values in the effort. On the voyage Wesley met a group of Moravians and became deeply impressed with their piety, particularly the confidence their faith gave them during the storms of ocean travel. Upon landing in America their bishop asked Wesley: "Do you know Jesus Christ?" Wesley could only answer that he knew Christ was the savior of the world and that he hoped Christ had died to save him. An inner assurance of salvation and an intimacy with Christ still eluded him.

The most famous incident in Wesley's life occurred on May 24, 1738, soon after his return from Georgia. He attended, unwillingly he said, the meeting of a religious society in Aldersgate Street where he heard someone reading from Martin Luther's preface to his commentary on Romans. As the passage described the change which God works in the human heart through faith in Christ, Wesley said that he felt his heart "strangely warmed." For the first time he said that he felt he really did trust Christ for his salvation and he knew that Christ had indeed taken away his sins and saved him from the law of sin and death.

Although this must have been an overpowering experience, and some have compared it with the conversion experiences of Paul and Augustine, Wesley mentioned it only once more in his writings. In fact, for the first six months after the experience, Wesley reported suffering from a spiritual depression. Apparently this was simply one of a number of important religious events in his life. It was, however, a confirmation of his call.

His preaching in churches usually ended with his being told not to preach there again, so he turned to the fields where workers and the poor were greatly moved by his sermons. His congregations were the new industrial masses. It is estimated that he traveled 225,000 miles and preached 40,000 sermons. He organized societies which were subdivided into classes and bands where small groups of people might learn together and help each other grow as Christians. Out of this came the structures of Methodism. Wesley never wanted to leave the Church of England. His desire was to promote renewal in it. In time, however, Methodism became a separate church.

ANTHONY BLOOM

We met Archbishop Bloom in the previous chapter. There we looked at some of his basic ideas about prayer. Later in his book, *Beginning to Pray,* he outlines a daily approach to prayer.

First, he says, when we awake in the morning we should thank God for the day.

Second, we should arise, wash, and do whatever we need to do to get ready for the day. Then we should come to God with two convictions: One is that we are God's own and the other is that the day is God's own, and absolutely new.

Third, we should ask God to bless the day and pray that everything in it should be ruled by God.

Fourth, we should go into the day as God's messengers. We are to be the presence of God, the Spirit, and the gospel in our encounters with other people. Sometimes we have to pay a high cost to represent God in this way. Still, every person and circumstance we meet should be seen as a gift from God.

Finally we need to rest from prayer; it's impossible to pray every minute. Better to single out a few occasions each day and put all of our energy into prayer. We will soon be defeated if we try to pray continuously. However, if we choose our prayer times intelligently we can have a rich prayer life.

SUMMARY

The six sources of this chapter all described ways of maintaining a schedule of prayer throughout the day.

The Didache

1. Fast on Mondays and Thursdays.
2. Pray the Lord's Prayer three times a day.

The Rule of St. Benedict

1. Love Christ above all else.
2. Maintain a balance between work, prayer, and reading.

3. Pray the psalms throughout the day.
4. Prayer should be brief, but frequent.

Lancelot Andrewes

1. Pray morning and evening.
2. Pay attention to scriptural teachings about prayer.
3. Develop a personal prayer book (to be discussed in chapter 7).

William Law

Pray five times each day on the following topics:

Morning prayer	Praise and thanksgiving
9:00 A.M.	Humility
Noon	Universal love and intercession
3:00 P.M.	Conforming to God's will
Evening prayer	Self-examination and confession

John Wesley

1. Items to be included in daily prayer:
   a. Deprecation.
   b. Petition.
   c. Thanksgiving.
   d. Intercession.
2. Pray for an hour in the morning and an hour in the evening.
3. The duty of a Christian:
   a. The renunciation of self.
   b. Devotion to God.
   c. Self-denial.
   d. Desiring nothing but God.
   e. Finding the reality of Christ living in us.
4. *A Scheme for Self-examination:*
   a. Morning and evening prayer.

    b. Brief ejaculatory prayers on the hour.
    c. Pray collects at 9:00 A.M., noon, and 3:00 P.M.
    d. Meditate at 6:00 P.M.
    e. Practice self-examination.
    f. Confess to each other.

Anthony Bloom

1. Upon waking, thank God for the day.
2. After dressing and preparing for the day, come to God believing:
    a. We are God's own.
    b. The day is God's and is new.
3. Pray that everything in the day be ruled by God.
4. Go into the day as God's messengers.
5. From time to time, rest from prayer.

So, we have seen six approaches to maintaining our prayer lives. Whether it is praying the Lord's Prayer three times a day as the *Didache* prescribed, praying on five different topics through the day as Law preferred, observing morning and evening prayer as Andrewes and Wesley did, or seeing every moment and situation as a gift from God as Bloom suggests, the idea is to be intentional about our prayer and to integrate it into our daily schedule as seriously as we would sleeping, eating, working, or the other things we do. While we may find Benedict's schedule impossible, his idea of praying the psalms as a way of deepening our prayer experience has merit and is something we ought to experience.

3

RULES FOR DEVELOPING A CONTEMPLATIVE ATTITUDE

It may be that having considered the first two chapters, you have come to see prayer as a deeper matter than just asking God for things you want. You also may have begun to develop certain disciplines, setting aside time on a regular basis for prayer. You now pray frequently, having integrated prayer into your normal routine. You are following all the rules. You offer prayers of praise, thanksgiving, confession and intercession. You have also begun to meditate on scripture and to ponder more carefully things you have often taken for granted or practiced by rote.

But still something is lacking. You are doing all the right things and making a sincere effort, often at the sacrifice of other elements that were once important in your life. However, God still seems very distant and, while you feel good about yourself for living a more disciplined religious life, you still wonder if there is something more that ought to be happening.

A serious spiritual life is more than just following the rules and doing things the proper way. More fundamental is the attitude with which we enter into and carry on our quest. In this chapter we will look at rules for developing the most important element in prayer, a contemplative attitude. What sort of perspective do we need in order to move into the deeper levels of prayer? What changes in our thinking and outlook must be made for an authentic encounter with the divine?

In this chapter we will look at two twentieth century spiritual writers who had much to say about the attitudinal preparation for prayer. Although both had an interest in rules for praying, they did not see specific practices as answers to problems with prayer. The most important element was developing a contemplative attitude.

EVELYN UNDERHILL

If asked to name an outstanding woman spiritual writer in the twentieth century, one would surely have to include the name of Evelyn Underhill in the list. Her great work, *Mysticism,* is a major study of the history and psychology of Christian mysticism, and her many other books and articles have opened the subject of spirituality for many.

The daughter of an English barrister, she was born in 1875 and studied botany and history at King's College of the University of London. Travel abroad contributed to her education, and she early showed the capacity for self-study and research. She began her literary career as a writer of poetry and novels, her best work probably being *Column of Dust,* published in 1909. From that point on, however, she concentrated her work in the area of spirituality.

The marriage to a childhood friend, Hubert Stuart Moore, gave her financial security and the leisure to pursue her mystical interests. She had planned to become a

Roman Catholic, but in the year of her marriage, 1907, the papacy condemned Modernism, a movement of which she considered herself a part. For a number of years she lived outside the church, but eventually found her way into the Anglican communion.

The publication of *Mysticism* in 1911 established her as a major literary figure. It was an interpretative rather than a scholarly study, and went through twelve revised editions. She believed that mystical experience is a fact of human existence. It is a life process which results in the transformation of the person and union with God.

She did not believe that the mystical life ignored the active life in the world. Under the influence of her spiritual director, Friedrich von Hugel, she worked in the slums of North Kensington. He insisted that the mystical life was not a flight from reality, but a powerful influence on how one lives in the world. She came to see that one's spiritual life must impact every relationship: politics, science, industry, art, our attitudes toward nature and other people. In the early years of World War II, for example, she held to an unpopular pacifist position.

She was the first woman to be an outside lecturer at Oxford, the first woman to give retreats in the Anglican Church, a fellow at King's College and recipient of an honorary Doctor of Divinity degree from the University of Aberdeen. She was described as easily approachable and able to cross English class lines. However, she also enjoyed an active social life and entertaining.

Her work was not without its critics. She was seen as a popularizer, influenced by others. However, some think that she was a major factor in sustaining Anglican spirituality in the years between the two world wars. Her books are still reprinted today, and numerous doctoral dissertations have been written about her.

In 1915 she published a fine little book called *Practical Mysticism.* It was intended as a simple introduction to the mystical life and has a "how to" character about it. However, it is much deeper than just that. It focuses on the attitudinal preparation needed for an encounter with God.

In the book she uses the language of mysticism and refers to what we would call God as Absolute, Somewhat Other, Divine Reality, Ultimate Beauty, Being, Real, Eternal Wisdom, and Living Fact, among other terms. She defined mysticism as "the art of union with Reality." A mystic is someone who has attained that union to some degree or who seeks and believes that such union is possible. She was convinced that we know something only by uniting with it, by an interpenetration of it and ourselves.

One seeking union with God must make preparations. The first step, said Underhill, is self-simplification. This involves the purification of the senses and the purification of the will. The windows of our senses, she said, are smeared by such things as thought, convention, and self-interest. These cause us to see things as we want to or as an ideological commitment causes us to see them. We create images in our consciousness which allow us to interpret things, and these self-created images prevent us from seeing reality as it really is. It is not easy to perceive without interpreting, but this is a skill we must develop if our perceptions of reality are to be clear.

Another element of preparation is recollection. Underhill defined recollection as "the subjection of attention to the control of the will." She suggested a little exercise to help us develop this capacity. We should take some idea or simple object, such as a flower, and hold it before our minds for a period of time. In doing this we will have to resist all distractions. We will be attacked by boredom, by feelings of inadequacy, and our attention will wander. The first quarter of an hour, she said, will be absolute warfare as we learn how little control our will has over our attention.

However, she believed that in time we will begin to change. As we surrender to the influence of the object of our meditation, it will begin to exhibit "unsuspected meaning, beauty, and power." Ultimately we will have communion with it and begin to sense oneness with it. The assaults of the outside world will become less powerful and we will have a new sense of freedom. We will reorient ourselves to what is real and will cease being enslaved to the verb "to have."

The next step is to see contemplation as an act of love, of wooing God rather than critically analyzing Divine Reality. We will feel a desire to seek, to touch, to taste, rather than to consider and analyze. We will notice a tendency to give up ourselves in the search for God.

These developments will not occur overnight. Our growth will be gradual. Our communion with other things, an increase in the spirit of love, and overcoming the barriers which individuality creates, will not come suddenly, but after a period of effort. What will happen, however, is what Underhill called an "enlargement of boundaries." We will begin to see that all things are related, that there is a oneness to reality. She reported that the great mystics could only say about their experience that the world is "unwalled."

In *Practical Mysticism* Underhill outlined three forms of contemplation. The first is that of finding God in the natural world. We begin by loving those manifestations of life that we see around us: the beauty of nature, of other people. We perceive God's presence in the sense world.

The second form of contemplation involves looking beyond the visible world. We recognize, as Julian of Norwich said, that God made it, loves it, and keeps it. Everything, whether we think it is benevolent or malignant, is wrapped in love. We realize that matter is not evil. It is difficult for us to see God because of our need for images, and Underhill quoted the unknown fourteenth century author of *The Cloud of Unknowing* who said that we know God by loving, not by thinking. Now we plunge into an imageless silence and begin to understand the Psalmist who wrote, "Be still and know that I am God" (Psalm 46:10).

The third form of contemplation is different from the first two in that it does not require effort on our part. It requires a letting go of self-interest, even of the most spiritual kind, so that what she called the "forces of the spiritual world" can work on us. After serious preparation, it is this letting go that enables us to sense more clearly the inexhaustible riches of the Ultimate Reality we call God.

If this discussion seems a bit vague, let me suggest another item by Evelyn Underhill that comes as close to a personal rule as anything she wrote—a little pamphlet she composed for the YWCA in 1926 simply called "Prayer." She lamented that many people go through life without ever knowing all that prayer can be for them. The usual excuse is a lack of time, but it is the failure to develop a life of prayer that makes our lives so frantic in the first place. She defined prayer as "communion with God," a way of developing friendship with the divine. Prayer means realizing that there is no place where God is not.

Christ, she wrote, made three promises about prayer: we will receive that for which we ask, we will find what we seek, and if we knock on the door we will be received into the kingdom of heaven. Simply "saying our prayers" routinely gives up these possibilities.

She called real prayer "a great and difficult art," one that requires continuing education and practice. The body requires a good diet, fresh air, and exercise to be healthy. So does the soul. It will only function well if it is in good spiritual health. We need a good diet of the most nourishing thoughts about God we can find. We do not need trivial religious ideas or sweetmeats, but what she called "the bread of life without too much butter on it."

Underhill made three suggestions. First, we get spiritual food through doing some reading and meditation every day. She encouraged the reading of the Bible, especially the New Testament and psalms, as well as the great spiritual classics, such as the *Imitation of Christ*. These give us "real news about God," and prevent our prayer from becoming superficial and monotonous. It is important that we learn from those who know more about God than we do.

Second, the equivalent of fresh air is an awareness of the greatness, splendor and gentleness of God. We need to develop a sense of wonder about God, to be awestruck at the reality of God's unchanging and universal presence. As this attitude becomes more habitual our spiritual vitality will increase.

Third, the exercise which our souls need is the discipline of regular prayer whether we feel like it or not. Regular persevering prayer keeps us spiritually fit. Regular corporate worship is also important in maintaining spiritual fitness.

These things must be done steadily if we are to benefit from them. Underhill recommended adopting a simple rule for prayer, reading, self-examination, and public worship, and sticking with it at all costs.

What then, should be the character of our prayer? Underhill felt that prayer which simply asked God for things or gave thanks for things received reflected a "mean, ungenerous, self-interested outlook." Deeper prayer involves adoration, "a self-forgetful, outflowing worship of God in His greatness and beauty; and a close, confident, dependent clinging to Him, never departing in thought or act from His presence in our souls."

The Lord's Prayer, for example, asks for little. It prays that God's name will be hallowed, that God's kingdom will come, that God's will be done. It is a prayer of one who has forgotten self. She reminds us that when Isaiah saw God in the temple, he did not ask for anything, but only offered himself.

All of this is to produce a life in which even the most simple things we do have about them the quality of worship. Then life becomes a "resolute attending to God."

THOMAS MERTON

Evelyn Underhill wrote in the first half of the twentieth century. Thomas Merton may well have been the most popular and widely read spiritual writer of the second half of the century. Thousands, perhaps millions, of people have been influenced by his life and thought and led to deeper faith and intimacy with God. Like many of the great saints of the church, his conversion marked a radical change in life, and his considerable literary talents came to be used in the service of spiritual guidance.

Merton did not write a personal rule for prayer. Indeed, he would have opposed a rigid system of devotion. However, he did have much to say about how we ought to approach prayer, and his thoughts might serve as a corrective for some of the other ideas presented in this book.

Merton was born in France in 1915 where his parents, both artists, happened to be painting at the time. His father was from New Zealand. His mother, an American Quaker, died when he was six years old. Spending much of his early life with grandparents at Douglaston, New York, Merton occasionally traveled with his father to Bermuda and France. In 1929 they went to England where his father died from a brain tumor. His younger brother, John Paul, would later be killed in World War II, leaving him with no immediate family. A godfather who served as guardian introduced Merton to modern art and literature and contributed significantly to his intellectual formation. In 1933 he entered Clare College in Cambridge, but lived to the extreme the life of a dissipated undergraduate, causing his godfather to urge him to return to his grandparents in New York. He enrolled in Columbia University and studied literature. In spite of his continued hard-drinking life of self-indulgence, he managed to complete a B.A. and M.A. with a thesis on William Blake. A Ph.D. dissertation on Gerard Manley Hopkins was never completed.

During his graduate study he converted to Roman Catholicism and, after an aborted attempt to become a Franciscan, entered, in 1941, the Abbey of Gethsemani in Kentucky, a Cistercian monastery. The Cistercians, popularly called Trappists, were known for the rigor of their austere life, characterized by solitude, silence, and self-denial. It was a radical change in life-style for

Merton, but a change which ultimately benefited many Christians who would read about his thoughts and experiences in the monastery. His best-selling autobiography, *The Seven Storey Mountain,* expressed all the enthusiasms of a new convert, describing his life through the early years at Gethsemani. In time, Merton would become more ecumenical in his outlook, not only toward other Christian groups, but toward some non-Christian religions as well. He was particularly interested in Zen Buddhism, Sufi mysticism, and Hinduism, although never losing his commitment to Christianity.

The last three years of his life at Gethsemani were spent in a hermitage in the monastery woods with brief contacts with the monastery community. Interestingly enough, however, Merton was also a social critic and wrote frequently in his later life expressing opposition to the nuclear arms race, the war in Viet Nam, and racism. He died in 1968 while visiting Asia, seeking an opportunity to talk to spiritual and monastic leaders of the east.

While he never wrote a personal rule such as many of those studied earlier in this book, he gave himself to a life characterized by many regulations. In fact, after it was decided he should not become a Franciscan, he bought a breviary and attempted to pray the offices daily as a layperson.

The *Rule* of St. Benedict was the foundation of Cistercian life, and the life of the monk was governed by regulations which prescribed daily schedule, diet, human relations, clothing, relations with the outside world, prayer, liturgy and, in Merton's case, publications. Those who knew him insisted that above all he was an obedient monk, but he did encourage reforms to make the Cisterican life both more humane and more contemplative.

Merton wrote some sixty books, and items that had not yet been published at his death are still appearing. *Contemplative Prayer,* published soon after his death, summarizes much of what he had to say about prayer, and would be a good source to consult in developing one's own rule for prayer. In this book he seemed to use the terms prayer and meditation interchangeably and even wrote of "meditative prayer." He saw contemplative prayer as a way of knowing God as opposed to knowing about God. In another of his books, *New Seeds of Contemplation,* he described contemplation as an awareness of God. "Contemplation," he said, "is always beyond our own knowledge, beyond our own light, beyond systems, beyond explanations, beyond discourse, beyond dialogue, beyond our own self." *Contemplative Prayer* was written for monks, but any Christian can find it useful.

Merton stated one of his foundational beliefs in the next to last chapter of *Contemplative Prayer.* Christianity, he said, is a religion for people who know that there is "a deep wound, a fissure of sin" that strikes at the very heart of our being. We are drawn to faith and to prayer because we know that something within us is not right, that somehow we are estranged from God. This deep wound in the human heart results in war, injustice, oppression, alienation, and a whole host of human problems. So we seek healing and turn to God. One of the ways we seek that healing which God offers is through prayer.

But it is not just God we are seeking, it is our own identity. Who are we? Merton said that we are a word spoken by God, and God does not speak words without meaning. Therefore, our true identity is hidden in God's call to us and our response. All of us, not just monks, need a certain amount of interior silence and discipline to maintain our human and Christian identity. Prayer brings us face-to-face with who we are. If we pray and find emptiness and dread, we have learned much about ourselves and what we need to do. Merton wrote that prayer is a "special way of following Christ." We share Christ's passion when we face our own emptiness and interior confusion. We share his resurrection when we become more deeply aware of who we are in God.

Merton also saw prayer as a way of resting in God who loves us, is near to us, and attracts us. This leads to an appreciation of silence and a realization of the futility of distractions and communications which add nothing to the simplicity of prayer.

For Merton, the method of prayer and meditation is not the key to deepening our awareness of God; it is attitude that makes the difference. There is no magical system. What counts are "faith, openness, attention, reverence, expectation, supplication, trust, and joy." These are the most important elements as we think about designing our own personal rule for prayer. Having a contemplative attitude is more important than the way or the number of times we pray. The New Testament, Merton pointed out, does not offer us techniques; it simply tells us to turn to God, depend on grace, and realize that the Spirit is given to us in Christ.

Prayer has what Merton called a paschal rhythm. Sometimes it is death when we recognize our own emptiness. At other times it is life, and God gives us new insight and awareness. When we get serious about prayer and begin to make progress, there is an inevitable letdown. Merton suggested that this may be the result of a neglect of the external world and not facing reality. One of the conditions for a fruitful inner life, he said, is

an openness to and love for others. These are stimuli for
the interior life, not dangers to it.

Authentic prayer introduces us to deep interior
silence and, hence, must always be simple. Often no
words or thoughts are used. Merton complained about
misplaced effort in the spiritual life that insists on maintaining compulsive routines rather than growing beyond
what he called our own short-sighted notions of prayer.
The purpose of prayer, he said, is to prepare the way for
God to develop within us "a capacity for inner illumination by faith and by the light of wisdom, in the loving
contemplation of God."

There are two important issues that Merton faced in
this book about which many Christians are confused.
One is the relationship between private and public
prayer. The other is the relationship between contemplative activity and doing good works in the world.

Public, or liturgical, prayer and private prayer should
form a harmonious unity. Each feeds the other. Communal
worship, said Merton, is blessed by "the presence of
Christ in the mystery of the worshipping community."
However, private meditative prayer is also essential to our
interior development. Merton called for a "full and many-
sided life of prayer in which all these things can receive
their proper emphasis." An authentic prayer life contains
both public and private elements, although the tendencies
in individual personalities must be respected.

The other issue, contemplation versus action, is one
that worries many well-intentioned Christians. Should
one spend energy on the inner life when there is so much
human suffering in the world that needs our attention?
Merton, referring to a comment by St. Bernard of
Clairvaux, noted that Mary and Martha were sisters and
should live in peace in the same house. The contempla-

tive, Mary, and the activist, Martha, are both essential elements in a well-balanced Christian life. Contemplation does not exclude action, but, for Merton, it does transcend action. Each of us needs to find the proper balance of action and contemplation for our own vocation. The gospel that calls us to action also calls us to intimacy with God. Prayer, said Merton, does not blind us to the world, but it enables us to see the world in the light of God.

Merton believed that self-denial and sacrifice were essential to serious prayer. Many of us resist this notion, but for Merton the purpose of self-denial was not to make the Christian life a cult of suffering; it was to make us free. He quoted Paul in 2 Corinthians 6:10 who said that he was treated "as sorrowful, yet always rejoicing; as poor, yet making many rich; as having nothing, and yet possessing everything."

This does not mean taking the world less seriously or having a contempt for the material world. It is, rather, a matter of freedom and detachment from "inordinate cares," the ability either to sacrifice or to use things in the service of love. Self-denial was a major characteristic of the monastic life and especially the Cistercians. However, Merton said that exercises such as fasting or other forms of denial will not accomplish anything unless the motive for doing them comes from personal meditation. If they are purely formal or done to free an anxious ego, they are better left undone. It would be better to eat a full meal in a spirit of gratitude than to give up some small part of it and regard that as a martyrdom. Prayer and sacrifice, said Merton, must work together. Without one there will not be the other.

A final topic which Merton spent a good bit of time discussing must be mentioned, and that is the experience of the dark night of the soul. We have been making

progress in our prayer lives, growing in our sense of intimacy with God, when suddenly our prayer becomes dry.
The progress we have made is lost, and we wonder if we
have been deceiving ourselves about faith and our relationship with God. We are deprived of the light and consolation we have been seeking. It is tempting to stop
praying and to give up faith. This can be a terribly painful
and frustrating time for the seriously religious person.

Merton, however, saw the dark night experience as
a positive development. It represents the transfer of our
inner life into the hands of God. The reason this experience is described as darkness is that God is present without any images, without any mental representation.
There is no way that we can conceptualize God in our
minds. What is happening is that we are being purified
or emptied of inadequate concepts and images of God so
that we may get rid of immature ways of prayer. We are
forced to face the truth of our emptiness, and our faith
will be tested.

If we understand what is happening in the dark
night we will realize that the knowledge of God is not
the knowledge of an object by a subject, but a matter of
losing ourselves in God. We recognize the loss of our
own autonomy and sense that we belong to God. As
Merton said, "The infinite God has no boundaries and
our minds cannot set limits to him or to his love." As
soon as we try to verify the presence of God, God eludes
us. The knowledge of God is far different from scientific
knowledge, and the realization of this mystery marks a
major breakthrough in our spiritual growth. So, darkness
can bring us enlightenment and growth if we realize that
in that darkness we are closer to God than before. The
point of meditation and prayer, then, is not to arrive at
some kind of objective knowledge of God, but to realize

that our very being is penetrated with God's love for us and knowledge of us.

SUMMARY

How do we develop a contemplative attitude? Underhill and Merton made a number of useful suggestions.

Evelyn Underhill

1. Basic to a contemplative attitude:
   a. Self-simplification.
   b. Recollection—controlling attention with the will.
   c. Loving, rather than analyzing, God.
2. Forms of contemplation:
   a. Finding God in the natural world.
   b. Looking beyond the natural world to an imageless God.
   c. Letting the forces of the spiritual world work on us by letting go of self-interest.
3. Daily prayer:
   a. Do some spiritual reading and meditation every day.
   b. Have a sense of wonder about the greatness, splendor, and gentleness of God.
   c. Pray regularly and participate in corporate worship.

Thomas Merton

1. Our true identity is hidden in God's call to us and our response.

2. Having a contemplative attitude is more important than the way or number of times we pray.
3. A fruitful inner life requires an openness to and love for others.
4. Authentic prayer leads to deep interior silence.
5. Liturgical and private prayer should form a harmonious unity.
6. Contemplation and action are both essential in a well-balanced Christian life.
7. Self-denial and sacrifice make us free for contemplative living.
8. The dark night of the soul represents the transfer of our interior life into the hands of God. It purifies us and leads to losing ourselves in God.

4

RULES FOR PRAYER AND SOCIAL ACTION

Thus far we have treated the spiritual life as if it were a solitary activity. The emphasis, for the most part, has been on personal prayer, meditation, and interior development. That, however, should not be seen as the only possible approach to knowing God. Evelyn Underhill, you may recall, wrote of loving those manifestations of life that we see around us. A writer of Genesis said that we were created in the image of God. To me that means that we can find God in other people.

It may be that an interior approach to spirituality is not appropriate for you if you are an extrovert, a people person. In that case you might begin to look for God in community, in the relationships between people, in human encounters.

In this chapter we will look at two people who built their own spirituality that way. One is a woman, the other a man, and they developed the sensitivity to see the divine presence in other people.

DOROTHY DAY

Many people regard Dorothy Day as one of the saints of the twentieth century. A journalist by profession, she devoted most of her life to the service of the poor and hopeless. Her life was an example of a marriage of spirituality and social action.

She was born in 1897, the daughter of a sports writer. When she was six years old the family moved from Brooklyn to California where she experienced the San Francisco earthquake, an early encounter with human suffering that would have a long-term effect on her life. After that catastrophe the family moved to Chicago and, upon graduating from high school, Day enrolled in the University of Illinois. Although she had been exposed to religion through her friends, there was no family practice. A comment by one of her professors that strong people did not need religion confirmed her tendency toward secular social reform.

When her family moved to New York, she dropped out of college to rejoin them and pursue a career in journalism. Her father did not think it an appropriate field for women and instructed the editors he knew not to hire her. Consequently, she worked for a series of radical, socialist papers: the *Call,* the *Masses,* the *Liberator,* and the *New Masses.* She covered strikes, workers' protests, and the peace movement.

In 1917 she was arrested while picketing the White House for women's suffrage and served a thirty-day jail sentence. In her autobiography, *The Long Loneliness,* she described the experience as one of the great trials of her life. She and other inmates began a hunger strike and, in her pain, she read the Bible and prayed. When her term was over, however, she dropped all religious practice and interest.

In time she became an established part of the Greenwich Village literary and social avant-garde. She had friendships with some of America's leading literary figures as well as radical thinkers. Her life was a constant round of journalistic activity and long discussions on social issues in various New York taverns. From time to time, while returning home from all-night sessions with friends she would drop in at a local Catholic church. She had no idea what was going on in the mass, but did like the quiet atmosphere of worship.

There followed in her life nurse's training, a brief unfortunate marriage, the publication of a novel while writing for a New Orleans paper, and a common-law marriage with a biologist on Staten Island. Latent religious interests began to surface again when she became pregnant. She had the baby baptized, even though she knew that would end her relationship with the atheistic biologist, and she became a Catholic in December 1927.

She took a job as a script writer in Hollywood, but soon left it and went to Mexico where she wrote articles about the poor for a Catholic journal. Near the end of 1932 the journal sent her to Washington to cover the hunger march. It was in the depths of the Depression. While there she prayed to be shown a way to help the poor, and the prayer was answered when she returned to New York and encountered Peter Maurin waiting for her in her apartment.

Maurin was a French peasant who had once belonged to the Christian Brothers order. He had a deep interest in social and intellectual issues. Eventually leaving France he came to Canada and then the United States, working as a laborer just long enough to afford food. Otherwise, he spent his time reading in the New York Public Library and arguing social issues with whomever he could find around Union Square. He made it his mission to develop Dorothy Day's Catholic intellectual background. He instructed her in church history

and introduced her to the spiritual classics. Together
they began a monthly newspaper called *The Catholic
Worker*. Its purpose was to promote "radical social
action based on Christian principles." The first issue
appeared on May 1, 1933. It contained articles on unem-
ployment, trade unions, cooperatives, the exploitation of
blacks, child labor, and a local strike. The paper is the
world's best journalistic bargain; it costs a penny a copy
and is still published today.

Day and Maurin also established a "house of hospitality," a place where homeless people could get food,
used clothing, and occasionally shelter. Sometimes the
crowd broke out into fights and many visitors were
drunk or demented, but no one was turned away. She
was fond of quoting Father Zossima in *The Brothers
Karamazov*: "Love in practice is a harsh and dreadful
thing compared to love in dreams."

Dorothy Day never wrote a personal rule, but she did
describe her own prayer life in a regular column in the
Catholic Worker, which was called "On Pilgrimage." Her
spirituality was based on the parable of the last judgment
in Matthew 25 where Christ said that when we feed the
hungry, give drink to the thirsty, welcome the stranger,
clothe the naked, and visit the sick and imprisoned, we
are doing it to him. Those were all things that the Catholic
workers tried to do. When critics complained that such
work did not really solve any social problems, Day replied
that this was the work that Christ commanded.

Dorothy Day and the other Catholic workers lived
lives of voluntary poverty. They were completely dependent upon charity, received no government funds, and
refused even to become a tax-exempt institution. This,
they believed, would involve cooperation with the state
which would infringe upon their independence. Day

saw poverty both as a virtue and as a source of freedom and joy. She saw a difference between hopeless destitution and voluntary poverty. Voluntary poverty freed people from the oppression of an acquisitive society and enabled them to identify with the poor.

Day said that there were two things essential to the success of the Catholic Worker movement. First, she said, they must practice the presence of God, be aware of God's presence in their midst. Essential to this was daily attendance at mass. This was what gave her strength for the constant living with destitution. The mass emphasized sacrifice, prayer, adoration, contrition, thanksgiving, and supplication, and these things put life into perspective for her. She also saw value in the communal side of Christian spirituality. It was important that the Catholic workers share the life of worship together.

She also had an appreciation for the sensory element in worship, and this ought to be a consideration in our own personal rules. What use can we make of our five senses in increasing our awareness of God? Day wrote of the importance of music, incense, color, rich vestments, water, oil, the making of the sign of the cross as well as the beauty of nature. All of these things stimulated her awareness of God.

The other essential for Day was what she called indoctrination. By that she meant "giving a reason for the faith that is in us." One of the foundation stones of that faith was a belief in the fatherhood of God. God was the father, the parent, of every person. That is why she was interested in social problems, peace, the poor and the other concerns that appeared in the pages of the *Catholic Worker.* All people are related and ought to care for one another.

Part of her unwritten daily rule was reading the

Bible. In fact, in her old age she appealed for a large print Bible so she could continue reading it. In its pages Christ was present.

However, for Dorothy Day there was another primary source of revelation and that was the poor. She believed that when she offered food or shelter to the poor she was functioning as Lazarus, Martha, or Mary, and the guest was Christ. "When you did it to the least of these you did it to me."

In an article called "Room for Christ" which she published in the Christmas, 1945, issue of the *Catholic Worker*, she expressed her belief that Christ speaks through the voice of others. She admitted that it was sometimes very hard to see Christ in some people, such as the pestering, cursing drunk that came in the Catholic Worker house making demands on everyone. Nevertheless, she insisted that Christ was present in slum dwellers, factory workers, store clerks, the homeless as well as others, and that when we encounter them we are encountering Christ. No haloes appeared over people's heads, but that was not the way Christ was present. However, she was convinced that when we show hospitality to another person, we are showing it to Christ.

Prayer was very important for her. She believed that it was always answered in some way, even in the most desperate situations. For her it was as necessary to life as breathing. She called it her food and drink which brought health to the soul, and the soul needed exercise as much as the body.

Keeping a journal was one way of praying, she believed. Another was to pray the psalms in the Old Testament. The Catholic Worker community prayed the office of compline which used the psalms every evening. She herself prayed the psalms morning and evening. In addition, she prayed the Lord's Prayer three times a day on her knees.

Another form of prayer which interested her was the Jesus Prayer from the Eastern Orthodox tradition, mentioned earlier by Anthony Bloom. A simple prayer, "Lord Jesus Christ, have mercy on me," it has a long history and summarizes the gospel. It is described in a Russian spiritual classic, *The Way of a Pilgrim,* and Day found it particularly helpful in stressful situations. Sometimes, she said, the problems at the Catholic Worker house were so great that she could only bow her head to the storm and pray. The Jesus prayer, she said, helped her.

She did not see a life of prayer as a reclusive life. Rather, she saw it as preparation for the battle with the forces of evil in the world. She often said that one of the purposes of the Catholic Worker movement was to help create a world where it would be easier for people to be good. After praying together, Christians often go out into a hostile world of war, injustice, hunger, and a whole host of social problems. Deep prayer is preparation for dealing with those realities.

Serving the poor was not enough for Dorothy Day. That service had to be undergirded with prayer, worship, and a growing understanding of the gospel. For those of us who think we are too busy to pray, we should look at her life where the demands were so great and terrible. Even in the midst of a life of unending service, she found a way to pray.

DOM HELDER CAMARA

The second person who has much to teach us about finding Christ in others is a Brazilian Catholic bishop,

Dom Helder Camara. He has been one of the truly remarkable religious leaders of the Third World. A strong advocate for social justice and a critic of political and economic structures that keep people in poverty, he is another example of one who has combined a deep spirituality with an impressive social activism.

Camara was born in 1909 in a poor area of Brazil, entered the priesthood and moved through the ranks rapidly, developing expertise in the field of education. In 1952 he was named auxiliary bishop of Rio de Janeiro where he devoted himself to the problems of the *favelas,* the poverty-stricken shanty towns of that city. In 1964 he was made Archbishop of Olinda and Recife in his home area of Brazil.

Rather than live in the episcopal palace like his predecessors, he took up residence in a small room that had been the sacristy of a church. He lived very simply and tried to be open to everyone, especially the poor. His practice was to get up at 2:00 every morning and pray for two hours, then go back to bed for awhile. The days were so busy that this was his best prayer time.

His goal in these times of prayer was to restore a sense of unity in himself, a oneness with Christ. He believed that oneness with Christ produces oneness with other people. He also prayed the breviary regularly and believed that eucharistic prayer "envelops the whole day in wonder."

Like Dorothy Day, Archbishop Camara believed that at the last judgment we will be judged by how we have treated those who are hungry, thirsty, dirty, injured, and oppressed. He said that Christ is present in the persons of Jose, Antonio, Severino, and others who are seeking justice. We cannot love God, he said, without loving other people, especially that two-thirds of the human race who must live in subhuman conditions. This would mean giving up the privilege, power, and prosperity that many of us enjoy.

Camara believed that in the protests of the poor of the world the voice of God was speaking. It is not difficult to hear God's call today, he said. The difficulty is in responding to it. Christ is present, he insisted, in whoever is suffering, humiliated, and crushed as Christ himself was. The crucifixion is reenacted again and again in human suffering, and we can see Christ there. We do not need to go to Bethlehem to celebrate Christmas. All over the world people are being made into refugees and forced to have children in hovels. And Christ is born again.

This kind of spirituality is a powerful one. While it is relatively easy to isolate ourselves in a prayer closet, finding Christ present in other people confronts us with human realities we would rather not have to face. But God does not let us off that easily. We need to develop the sensitivity to the divine image in every person, to see Christ in others. Then the presence of God will become emphatic for us.

Spirituality is dangerous. I suspect we are often reluctant to pray because we are fearful of what an encounter with God might produce. We might hear God saying to us, sell what you have and give to the poor. In light of that it is easier to say we do not have time to pray or we have theological problems with prayer or prayer does not accomplish anything. In designing our own personal rule we need to develop the sensitivity to see God present in other people. The impact of that on our relationships will be immense.

SUMMARY

Although neither Day nor Camara ever wrote a personal rule, their prayer life was built around a number of regular daily practices. They can be outlined as follows:

Dorothy Day

1. Practice the presence of God; be aware of God's presence.
2. Attend the eucharist daily.
3. Read the Bible regularly.
4. Look for Christ's presence in the poor.
5. Pray morning and evening, using the psalms.
6. Keep a journal.
7. Pray the Our Father three times a day.
8. Use the Jesus Prayer.

Dom Helder Camara

1. Pray when others are asleep. For Camara, this was 2:00 to 4:00 in the morning.
2. Listen for the voice of God in the poor.
3. See Christ in other people, especially those who suffer.
4. Be prepared to give up power, privilege, and prosperity.
5. Pray the breviary regularly.

RULES FOR PRAYER IN CRISIS

People often make the mistake of thinking that a good spiritual life will bring peace and serenity, freedom from cares, and calm warm feelings in the heart. That is not always the case. Most of us, at some time or other in our lives, will find ourselves in crisis. If we attempt to live the gospel in a world abounding in injustice, racism, war, and other problems, crisis situations are guaranteed. In times of great stress it is very tempting to give up our disciplines of prayer until our lives calm down again. How do we pray if our world comes apart, if we find ourselves in situations that overwhelm us and we are unable to cope?

In this chapter we will look at two people in the twentieth century who lived in terrible crises that resulted in their deaths. For both people prayer was important in facing crisis.

DIETRICH BONHOEFFER

Dietrich Bonhoeffer was one of the most important theologians of our century. His execution by the Nazis at the age of 39 cut short what might have been a brilliant theological career. Even so, his influence is still strong today.

He was born in 1906, one of eight children of a distinguished psychiatrist and professor at the University of Berlin. Surprising his family with a decision to study theology, young Bonhoeffer attended the universities of Tübingen and Berlin, completing his dissertation in 1927. He served as an assistant pastor in Barcelona to meet the practical experience requirement for ordination, and then came to the United States for a year of study at Union Theological Seminary in New York. He was impressed with the student community life, but felt that the level of intellectual activity was considerably below that of European universities. The students were more interested in practical issues than in theology.

In 1931, during the rise of Nazism, Bonhoeffer returned to Germany to become a university lecturer. Five years later the Nazi Minister of Education would remove him from that position. He also began to work in the ecumenical movement, an involvement that would soon become critical for him as he made contacts with church leaders across Europe and England.

When Hitler came to power in 1933, the Lutheran church in Germany was divided. The German Christians supported the new regime, but a minority of Lutherans formed the Confessing Church, a church which confessed that there was no higher authority than God. In 1935 Bonhoeffer organized an underground seminary in Finkenwalde to train ministers for the Confessing Church. The seminary was closed by the Gestapo two years later, and most of the students died in the war. It was during these years that Bonhoeffer wrote two of his most important books, *The Cost of Discipleship* and *Life Together.*

Life Together is a book about community life in the Christian fellowship, lived in the context of Nazism.

While Bonhoeffer discussed what a Christian community must do, he also had a chapter on "The Day Alone," and gave some suggestions useful for designing a personal rule. Solitude, he believed, was essential to good community life. Community life will not be fruitful unless the members also have some time alone. Even members of a family who live close together need periods of solitude and quiet.

Whereas speech is the mark of community, silence is what characterizes solitude. There are times of common worship and prayer when speech is necessary, but there should also be times of silence in the day. The word, said Bonhoeffer, comes not to one who chatters, but to one who is silent. He defined silence as "the simple stillness of the individual under the Word of God." We are silent before hearing the word because we want to listen to it and we are silent after hearing it because it is still speaking within us. We should be silent at the opening of the day so that God can have the first word, and be silent at the end of the day so that God will have the last word. True silence, he said, is the consequence of spiritual stillness. After we have been silent for a time, we meet the world and other people in a new and fresh way.

Bonhoeffer saw three purposes of solitude: meditation, prayer, and intercession. God requires these of us.

Meditation, said Bonhoeffer, lets us be alone with the word. In meditating on scripture, we should use only a brief text, perhaps using the same text for an entire week. In community we might read the entire Bible together, but in solitude we go into the depths of a particular sentence or word. We choose a passage in the faith that it will have something personal to say to us on a given day, that it will be not only God's word for the church, but God's word for us individually. Here, however, we are not concerned about what the text says to others, but what it says to us.

We often enter meditation burdened with many thoughts, concerns, and images that distract us, and it may take some time before the word of God breaks through and becomes clear to us. We need not meditate on the whole text we have chosen; one word might be enough. Even expressing our thoughts in words is not necessary. Unphrased thoughts and prayers may be more appropriate in meditation. It is not necessary to search for new ideas in meditation. The point is to let God's word work within us.

As many other spiritual writers have discovered, there may well be times of spiritual dryness when meditation is difficult, if not impossible. We may not always have elevating and fruitful experiences of meditation. The point is to center our attention on the word itself, not upon any "experiences" we may hope to have. The promise of the gospel is that if we seek God alone, we will gain happiness.

Good meditation should lead to prayer. Bonhoeffer recommended that our prayer be guided by scripture. This way our own emptiness will not frustrate our prayer. He wrote a fine little book called *Psalms: The Prayer Book of the Bible* in which he called the Psalter "the great school of prayer." We may find some of the psalms imprecatory, vengeful and bitter, but Bonhoeffer saw these as the psalms of Christ who knew suffering, pain, and injustice. This makes the Psalter "the prayer book of Jesus in the truest sense of the word," and when we pray the psalms we are praying with Jesus and he becomes our intercessor.

Bonhoeffer saw prayer as a readiness to receive the

word in our personal situations with all of their problems, temptations, sins, and decisions. What we cannot
pray in the community we can make known to God
silently. On the basis of a word of scripture we pray for
many things: the clarification of the day, freedom from
sin, growth in holiness, strength for our work. Prayer is
heard when it is a response to God's promise.

Bonhoeffer knew that in prayer and meditation our
thoughts often wander. However, we should not let this
problem defeat us. Rather than trying determinedly to
prevent it, we should calmly incorporate into our prayer
those things which cause our thoughts to stray.

Intercession, the third purpose of solitude, involves
praying for people who are committed in some way to
our care. Each of us has our own circle of people who
have requested our prayers. We need to pray for those
we live with day by day. A Christian fellowship, said
Bonhoeffer, lives by the intercessions of its members for
each other or it collapses. Furthermore, we cannot con-
demn or hate those for whom we pray. In intercession,
another person becomes one for whom Christ died.
Intercession, for Bonhoeffer, means to bring another into
the presence of God and see that individual under the
cross of Christ as one in need of grace. So, intercession
is a daily service that we owe to God and to others.

Since the grace of God is found in meditation on
scripture, prayer, and intercession, and since these are
services we owe, it is important to set aside a regular
hour for them. This is not legalism, it is "orderliness and
fidelity." Our claim on this time is prior to the claims
others have on us. Bonhoeffer even suggested that a pastor's whole ministry will depend on it.

Our meditation is tested every day, for all of us must
spend some time in what Bonhoeffer called an un-

Christian environment. Remember that he wrote this in the context of Nazi Germany. The issue is whether meditation has lodged the word of God securely within us so that we can function as Christians in the world, even under the most terrible circumstances.

In 1939 Bonhoeffer began another sabbatical in America at Union Theological Seminary. However, from the moment of his arrival he was miserable and made a fateful decision to return to Germany, only a month after his arrival.

Already underway was a plot among some of the German high command against Hitler. Bonhoeffer became involved in the plot. In his ecumenical travels he attempted to make contacts with the Allies to inform them of the resistance movement and to ask them to stop the war if Hitler were overthrown. The Allies, however, had made the decision to pursue the war until Germany surrendered unconditionally. Two attempts were made on Hitler's life, both of which failed. Eventually, many of the conspirators were arrested and Bonhoeffer was taken to prison on April 5, 1943. Two years later he would be hanged by the Nazis.

During those years in prison he practiced a very disciplined spiritual life which we can read about in his letters collected under the title *Prisoner for God: Letters and Papers from Prison.* He tells us that he read the Bible regularly in the morning and evening, recited hymns to himself, and prayed the psalms daily, as he had done for years before his arrest.

At first, Bonhoeffer believed that he would be released for a lack of evidence, but as time went on it eventually became clear that this would not be the case. His early letters contain notes of hope. On Easter Sunday, soon after his arrest, he wrote that Good Friday and

Easter cause us to look beyond ourselves and think of the meaning of life and its suffering and events. He mentioned reading the Bible, especially the passion story and the letters of Paul. Before going to sleep he would recite hymns that he had memorized during the day and upon waking up he would read psalms and hymns. Later he reported that he was reading the Bible straight through from cover to cover and was currently in Job. He also reported that he was reading the psalms daily, that he loved them more than any book in the Bible.

In one letter he reported being in a prison cell between two men who had been condemned to death. He read the Apocalypse and the psalms to prepare himself for the worst. By now he had read through the entire Old Testament two-and-a-half times, and he was trying to compile some prayers for use in prison. When he finally realized that he was not going to be released, he wrote that no matter how bad a situation may be, there is always a way through to God.

At one point he confessed to being terribly homesick and that he was tempted to sleep later than his usual 6:00 A.M. and abandon his daily routine. But he knew that would be the first step to capitulation and he would lose his power to overcome tension.

Bonhoeffer believed that discipline was the source of freedom, hence the development of his own routine of prayer and study in prison. He realized that his own free act as a minister opposing Hitler had now brought him suffering. He said that for a brief moment he had enjoyed real freedom, but now it had been given back to God that God might "perfect it in glory."

In one of the last surviving letters of Bonhoeffer, written eight months before his execution, he said that in such times of crisis we should make a special point of including thanksgiving in our prayers. It was important not to be absorbed in the present moment. While God does not give us everything we want, God still remains Lord of the earth, still preserves the church, still hears our prayers, and still renews our faith.

All that we have a right to expect from God, Bonhoeffer wrote, is to be found in Jesus Christ. Therefore, it is important that we persevere in meditating on the life, teachings, suffering, and death of Jesus in order to learn what God promises and fulfills. To live close to God is newness of life, and in that situation we realize that danger can only drive us closer to God.

In February, 1945, Bonhoeffer was moved from the Gestapo prison in Berlin to Buchenwald and other places. While conducting a church service for prisoners in a temporary prison in a school house, two men came for him. Everyone knew what that meant. His last words to his fellow prisoners as he was being taken away to be executed were, "This is the end, for me the beginning of life." In life he showed us how to face death by maintaining the disciplines of prayer. His rules for prayer in crisis provide good guidance for us.

MARTIN LUTHER KING, JR.

Martin Luther King, Jr. was, without question, the leading American Christian social activist of the 1950s and 1960s. His ministry led to profound changes in American society, changes the nation is still attempting to digest. In 1964 he received the Nobel Peace Prize. Like Bonhoeffer, his efforts for justice cost him his life, and like Bonhoeffer, his own spirituality sustained him in crisis.

He was born in Atlanta in 1929, the son of a Baptist minister. He graduated from Morehouse College, Crozer Theological Seminary, and Boston University where he received a Ph.D. degree for a dissertation on Paul Tillich and Henry Nelson Weiman. In 1954 he became pastor of the Dexter Avenue Baptist Church in Montgomery, Alabama, expecting to live the life of a typical minister, preaching and giving pastoral care to his congregation. However, the next year a black woman, Rosa Parks, violated bus segregation laws in Montgomery by refusing to give up her seat to a white man. Upon her arrest, the black community organized a boycott of the city bus system in the hope that economic pressure would force a change in bus segregation laws. King was drawn into the leadership of the boycott, and at that point his life changed radically. In time he became the foremost black leader of the civil rights movement. He organized the Southern Christian Leadership Conference and found himself having to work his way through the intricacies of black church politics, the American judicial system, southern culture, and the federal government. From time to time he was arrested and jailed, and he lived with constant threats on his life and the lives of members of his family.

In his book, *Stride Toward Freedom,* he expressed his belief that there was a moral force at work in the universe moving to overcome injustice. God is still at work in history and in the events of the civil rights struggle.

King wrote occasionally of his own religious experience. Well known is his statement: "I have been to the mountaintop and I have seen the promised land." Less well known is an incident from the Montgomery experience. One of King's main functions in the boycott was conducting weekly mass meetings at which he tried to offer encouragement and hope and arouse the flagging enthusiasm for the effort. As months went by and the city refused to make any change at all in bus segregation policy, people became discouraged. Many were tempted to give up the boycott which had caused them hardships in getting to work each day. In addition, King received constant death threats. He feared for the safety of his family. He reached a point of exhaustion and his courage, he said, was almost gone. He sat at his kitchen table and prayed. He confessed to God that he did not know if he could provide the leadership the movement needed. Fear had taken away his energy.

He reported that in that moment of surrender he sensed the presence of God as he had never known it before. He believed that he was being told to stand up for righteousness and truth and God would be with him. His fear and uncertainty disappeared, and he felt ready to face anything. Several days later, while he was out of town, his home was bombed. His wife heard something hit the front porch. She took the children and ran out the back while the front of the house was blown away. King later said that his religious experience several nights earlier enabled him to accept the news of the bombing calmly and gave him the strength to face it.

When bus integration finally came to Montgomery, King drew up some rules which were passed out all over the city. They urged people to continue practicing nonviolence, and included advice to uphold each other's commitments with prayer. If anyone saw a person being molested on a bus that person was to "pray for the oppressor and use moral and spiritual force to carry on the struggle for justice."

In *Stride Toward Freedom,* King listed his philosophical foundations for nonviolence. These might serve as philosophical foundations for our own rules for living.

1. Nonviolent resistance to evil is not cowardly or passive. It actively opposes evil with persuasion rather than violence.
2. Nonviolent resistance attempts to win an enemy's friendship and understanding by awakening a sense of moral responsibility. It does not attempt to defeat or humiliate.
3. Resistance is always directed against the evil itself, not individuals.
4. Nonviolence requires one to accept the possibility of suffering without retaliation. The heart of the nonviolent approach was accepting violence without striking back.
5. Nonviolence also resists doing psychological violence to others, such as hate campaigns.
6. This philosophy assumes that the universe is on the side of justice and that right will ultimately prevail.

One of the closest things to a personal rule King wrote was a list of ten commandments that volunteers in a Birmingham demonstration in 1962 had to sign. It is found in King's book, *Why We Can't Wait.*

1. Meditate daily on the teachings and life of Jesus.
2. Remember always that the nonviolent movement in Birmingham seeks justice and reconciliation—not victory.
3. Walk and talk in the manner of love, for God is love.
4. Pray daily to be used by God in order that all might be free.
5. Sacrifice personal wishes in order that all might be free.

6. Observe with both friend and foe the ordinary rules of courtesy.
7. Seek to perform regular service for others and for the world.
8. Refrain from violence of fist, tongue, or heart.
9. Strive to be in good spiritual and bodily health.
10. Follow the directions of the movement and the captains of a demonstration.

Those would be good rules for any Christian to observe. King knew the value of organizing one's life for the accomplishment of serious purposes.

In the midst of a community or personal crisis, it is important to have guidelines to follow when chaos threatens. Thinking ahead and preparing for crisis in time of calm can be of enormous help when we find ourselves in situations where there is no time or surplus energy to make fundamental decisions. If we are in the habit of following disciplines like those Bonhoeffer practiced and King taught, we will already be formed into people who can function well in crises.

SUMMARY

Both of these people had rather definite rules for prayer:

Dietrich Bonhoeffer

From the underground seminary experience:
1. Take time for solitude.
2. Provide times of silence for:
   a. Meditation on scripture; being alone with the word.

b. Prayer.
    (1) for clarification of the day
    (2) for freedom from sin
    (3) for growth in holiness
    (4) for strength for work
c. Intercession—pray for people committed in some way to our care:
    (1) for the people with whom we live
    (2) for our circle of friends
    (3) for members of the Christian fellowship
d. Thanksgiving—looking beyond the present moment

From the prison experience:

1. Reading the Bible morning and evening.
2. Pray the psalms daily.
3. Recite hymns.
4. Maintain the daily routine rather than giving in to weakness which causes a loss of power.
5. Make a special point to include thanksgiving in prayers, even in the worst situation. This enables us to look beyond the present moment.
6. Meditate constantly on the life, teachings, suffering and death of Jesus.

Martin Luther King, Jr.

1. Meditate daily on the life and teachings of Jesus.
2. Live in the manner of love.
3. Pray daily to be used by God.
4. Sacrifice personal wishes.
5. Perform regular service for others.
6. Stay in good bodily and spiritual health.
7. Pray for the oppressor.

RULES FOR SOLITUDE

A good friend who lived a hermit life for nine-and-a-half years wrote to me from his hermitage and said: "Everyone needs some time alone, time to ponder and dwell with things and let things be." This friend is now living in a community again, but his advice still holds true. Each of us needs to get away from the normal routine to ponder things, look inward, and take stock of ourselves.

Solitude, however, is not a friendly companion for many of us. When left alone we are sometimes confronted with boredom, lethargy, and aimlessness. Yet if used properly, solitude can be deeply enriching and can bring to our prayer lives stimulation and progress. The secret is knowing how to use it.

Many people have arranged to go on solitary retreats for a few days, but have been frustrated by the experience because of a lack of direction. Some, for reasons of health, age, or other circumstances are forced to live alone and have little contact with others. In this chapter I would like to present two people, one from the twelfth century and one from our own time. Both saw great value in solitude and provided guidance on how to use it.

Throughout the history of Christianity there have been many forms of solitude practiced. We have already looked at an example of the desert father and mother tradition. Others adopted the life of the recluse, a person who would spend a lifetime in a small cell. The fact that church councils in the fifth, sixth, and seventh centuries approved rules for recluses would indicate that the practice was not uncommon.

The most bizarre form of the life occurred in the Middle Ages when the recluse would enter a small room in a church after which masons would brick up the door. This life was chosen voluntarily, but it was a severe form of solitude. One of the most famous recluses was Julian of Norwich, an English recluse whose *Revelations of Divine Love* is a spiritual classic.

AELRED OF RIEVAULX

One of the great figures in twelfth century English spirituality was a Cistercian monk, Aelred of Rievaulx. Born around 1110, he eventually entered the monastic life and in 1147 became the Abbot of Rievaulx, a monastery not far from York. Among his best known writings are *The Mirror of Charity* and *On Spiritual Friendship*. In addition he wrote many sermons, treatises, and lives of saints.

Aelred had a sister who was a recluse, living in a small enclosed cell in a church. We know practically nothing about this woman. Fearful that she might sin, she asked Aelred to write a rule for her, as well as other young women who had taken up the life, to follow. Although by the very nature of things it is hard to imagine a recluse getting into too much trouble, it was an unnatural way of life. Boredom and depression were the great enemies. A confused mind made it difficult to concentrate on prayer, meditation, or reading. It was important to have the day well ordered. Consequently, Aelred composed his *Rule for the Life of a Recluse*.

The *Rule* had many sources. Part of it was based on the daily schedule and dietary regulations of the *Rule* of St. Benedict. Other sources were the writings of major church fathers, such as Jerome, Ambrose, Augustine, and Gregory. It was one of the earliest English rules for recluses, and was an influence on the later *Ancrene Riwle*.

Aelred's *Rule* had three parts to it:

1. The Outer Person
2. The Inner Person
3. The Threefold Meditation

The first part described the daily schedule and activities of the recluse. The second covered the interior attitudes. The last section encouraged meditation on the past, present, and future.

Aelred said some Christians chose solitude because living in a crowd could mean ruin. The desert fathers and mothers lived alone in the desert "to avoid ruin, to escape injury, to enjoy greater freedom in expressing their ardent longing for Christ's embrace." Others found the desert life an opportunity for aimless wandering and chose instead the "completely enclosed cell with the entrance walled up." That is the life his sister had chosen.

However, there were dangers even in this confining type of life. Aelred described the recluse who spent her days at her window gossiping and laughing about scandal. Then, "like a drunkard, she staggers through the psalms, gropes through her reading, wavers while at prayer," and the hermit life is ruined. Moreover, the recluse must avoid beggars at her window. If she had enough to give away she had too much and was no nun. Silence, said Aelred, is the first essential of the reclusive life. This is where she will find real peace. If she imposes silence on her tongue, her spirit will be free to speak. In silence, said Aelred, "she is with Christ, and he would not care to be with her in a crowd." She may, however, speak with a priest for confession or spiritual direction, although she should never touch him. Above all, she should maintain "her peace of heart and tranquillity of spirit, so she shall have ever dwelling in her soul the Lord."

Aelred assumed the schedule of canonical hours in the *Rule* of St. Benedict as the basic structure of the day. From the Exaltation of the Holy Cross (September 14) until Lent, the recluse is to be silent from compline, usually sunset, until dawn. After prime, six o'clock in the morning, she could give her attendant directions for the day, but should then refrain from further speech until terce, or nine o'clock in the morning. Between terce and none, or three o'clock in the afternoon, she could speak to callers and give further orders to her attendant. After none, having finished dinner, she should observe silence until vespers. From afternoon vespers until her evening light meal she may again talk to her attendant.

During Lent she should keep silence all day, although Aelred would allow her to speak with her attendant or confessor if absolutely necessary. Then, from Easter until September 14 she should remain silent from compline until dawn. She can speak to her attendant after prime and with visitors from none until vespers. After vespers communication with her attendant is again allowed.

Otherwise, how was the recluse to spend her time? Quoting from the *Rule* of St. Benedict that "idleness is the enemy of the soul," Aelred prescribed the hours for manual labor, reading, and prayer. His basic method was to alternate these three activities. When any one becomes a burden, the recluse should change to another. The psalms should be read until she grew tired of them. Then, she should read for a while. When tired of that, she should pray, and when wearied of praying, manual labor was prescribed.

Aelred gave some excellent advice on prayer. He suggested brief prayers for fear that prolonged effort might produce a distaste for it. It is better, he said, to pray briefly and often, unless the inspiration of the moment should prolong it. The basic schedule he outlined began with rising after midnight and reciting the office of vigils followed by prayer and the commemorations of the saints. After that the time should be used for reciting the psalms and manual work. At dawn she should recite the offices of lauds and prime. Until the next office, terce, she should divide her time between reading, prayer, and reciting the psalms. From terce until none, roughly six hours, she would do manual labor. Many recluses were seamstresses or did weaving in their cells. After dinner and until vespers she should alternate between spiritual exercises and manual work. After vespers she should read from the *Lives of the Fathers,* then say compline and go to bed "with her heart filled with love."

Aelred took fasting very seriously, especially during Lent. This, for him, was the preeminent fast period of the year. He called it "a shield no temptation can pierce." It is an essential part of the religious life; and the best protection for chastity.

The last topic of this first section of Aelred's *Rule*

concerned the recluse's diet. He prescribed the basic Benedictine diet of a pound of bread and half a bottle of wine, but encouraged abstaining from wine if possible. The basic principle was to satisfy hunger without gratifying the appetite. In addition, Aelred allowed one portion of either green vegetables or beans or porridge. For supper a very small portion of fish or a milk dish was allowed to which could be added fresh vegetables or fruit if available. During Lent the recluse should have only one meal a day, and on Friday she should fast on bread and water. With food, as with clothing, the good recluse should always have just a little less than she might lawfully be allowed. He concluded this section, "I have offered you a rule of life which, while tempered to the needs of the weak, allows the strong every opportunity of advancing to a greater perfection."

The second part of the *Rule*, "The Inner Person," is basically a treatise on virginity, considered the highest virtue in the Middle Ages. For our purposes, one of the exercises Aelred prescribed that is worth using was the examination of conscience. He suggested that when the recluse goes to bed she should go over the day and determine whether the Lord has been offended by any word, deed or desire. Has there been too much indulgence in food or drink, or has the recluse been heedless, idle, or negligent? If so, she should sigh over such lapses, repent of them and so, "reconciled to your Bridegroom by this evening sacrifice, go to sleep."

The reading of scripture was also suggested as a means of fighting temptation. "Nothing is better for preventing useless ideas or driving out impure imaginations than the study of God's Word," wrote Aelred. The recluse should be thinking over the scriptures when she goes to sleep and when she wakes up in the morning.

Part III, "The Threefold Meditation," recommended meditating on the past, present, and future. By the past, Aelred meant meditating on the life and ministry of Christ, from the annunciation through the resurrection. Meditating on the present means that the recluse should think about her own sins and how the grace of God overcomes them. Finally, she must meditate on the future, that is, on her own death. Death, said Aelred, will be the beginning of eternal happiness if she is properly ready. She should imagine herself standing before Christ's judgment seat and finally having the vision of God.

It is unlikely, perhaps not even desirable, that many will take up the solitary life today. However, there are a number of items in Aelred's *Rule* from which we can profit. The idea of a well-ordered day, the alternation of various spiritual exercises, the advice to pray frequently but briefly, and the value of a nightly examination of conscience, are all appropriate for any Christian. When solitude is frustrating, variety of activity may be healing.

CATHERINE DE HUECK DOHERTY

Most of the Rules we have examined thus far have come out of the western tradition of Christianity. Now we will summarize a devotional practice of the eastern Christian, specifically the Russian, tradition. Although raised as a Catholic by her parents, Catherine de Hueck Doherty grew up in Russia and was deeply influenced by that style of Christianity. Since coming to the west she has written a number of books describing basic principles of Russian spirituality.

Catherine Doherty is another example of someone who combined a deep spirituality with a strong social concern. She was born into a wealthy family in Russia in

1900. She wrote in one of her books, *Strannik*, that she saw her future as marriage, children, and farm life in the country. She did marry Baron Boris de Hueck at the age of fifteen. However, World War I and the Communist revolution altered the future for her. She and her family, with only the clothes on their backs, fled to Finland, then to England and, ultimately, Canada. Her husband worked as an architect, but was in poor health. The marriage was annulled and eventually he died, leaving Catherine with feelings of intense loneliness. She supported her young son working as a laundress, maid, waitress, and sales clerk. Eventually, she joined a lecture bureau and, in time, rose to an executive position. She was now financially secure and comfortable, lecturing across the United States and Europe.

Her faith was deep, however, and she increasingly pondered the words of Jesus: "Sell what you have, give it to the poor, and come follow me." In 1930 she talked to Archbishop McNeil of Toronto about whether these words were directing her to a new vocation. The archbishop suggested that she wait a year, pray about it, and if she still wanted to embrace poverty, he would support her. A year later she sold everything she had and, after reserving funds for her son's education, the two of them moved to the slums of Toronto. There she founded Friendship House to serve the poor. Several people joined her, but her manner and style produced misunderstanding, and she moved to Harlem in New York, starting another Friendship House in absolute poverty, serving the needs of the poor in that neighborhood. Among those who worked with her temporarily was Thomas Merton. She wanted to put life into the social teachings of the Catholic Church, but many had trouble understanding her vision of service.

In 1943 she married a journalist, Eddie Doherty, who shared her vision and, in 1947, they moved to Combermere, a village north of Toronto where the bishop had invited her to establish a ministry. Once again people came to join her, including several priests. The new ministry was called Madonna House. By 1975, when her book *Poustinia* was published, there were 125 full-time members and twelve missions. In 1955 she and her husband took vows of celibacy and he eventually was ordained in the Melkite Rite.

Poustinia is not a rule in the usual sense, but it does describe a devotional practice that has a long history in Russian Christianity. Those of us who live busy lives in the world could benefit from temporary retreats in a poustinia. Such a practice might become incorporated into our own personal rule.

A poustinia is a solitary place where one might go for a period of time on a regular basis. For some of us it might be just one day now and then, for others it might mean several days each week, or a longer period of time on a less frequent basis. The point is to find some time of solitude and silence for listening to God and the renewal and reorientation that brings. Doherty liked to go into her poustinia, an old farmhouse on the property of Madonna House, on Fridays.

Doherty believes that those of us who witness to Christ in the marketplace, in the world, need some periods of silence and solitude in our lives. True silence, she said, is the search for God. "Silence is holy," she wrote, "a prayer beyond all prayers, leading to . . . the heights of contemplation." Silence, however, is not a selfish thing. Doherty believed that it would generate a charity that results in the service of neighbor.

True silence, she believed, is not just an absence of

noise; it is listening to God. While having a poustinia to which we might retreat is valuable, the real poustinia, the real place of silence and solitude, is the human heart. To go into a poustinia means to listen to God, and we can develop the ability to do that almost anywhere.

Doherty describes an ideal poustinia in Chapter Four of the book. It should be very simple and stark. The room must be plain, containing a chair and a table with a Bible on it. There could be some writing paper and pencils. A basin and pitcher for washing could be provided. If there is a bed it should have wooden slats instead of a mattress, with a few blankets and pillow if necessary. Since a poustinia is also a place of fasting, there should be drinking water and a loaf of bread to be divided into three parts, one for each meal of the day. Hot water for tea or coffee could be acceptable. There should be a large plain cross on a wall and an icon with a vigil light. The plain cross is to remind us that Christ wants us to be crucified with him that we might share in his resurrection.

The poustinia is our spiritual desert. The desert has often been a symbol for poverty, austerity and simplicity. In the Bible it is often the place where God is encountered. We are alone with God and there is nothing to distract us except our own heart. In the poustinia we fast from both bodily and spiritual food, for the only book provided is the Bible where, Doherty believes, God is fully accessible.

The poustinia can be a fearsome place. When we are alone in it with nothing but God present we learn much about ourselves and our own interior poverty. Like Jesus in the desert, we may encounter a host of temptations. While the first few visits might seem exciting, in time we will experience boredom and dryness. Time will pass very slowly. This is because we resist turning ourselves completely over to God.

One of the main purposes for going into a poustinia is to receive a word from God. Often it will not come easily. Doherty describes some of her own experiences of restlessness and struggle. Sometimes it helps to take a nap. More than once she would wake up with a new word in her mind. Understanding what God is saying to us through that word can also be difficult, and the poustinia is a place to wrestle with that.

Catherine Doherty advises preparation for entering the poustinia. The day before we should begin to calm our minds, close our intellects and open our hearts. We should smile at everyone and be at peace. We should enter the poustinia with absolute simplicity. There is no daily schedule to follow such as Aelred prescribed for his sister the recluse. Rather, we should enter with simple hearts, knowing that from all eternity we are in the mind of God, even now. One of her favorite expressions is that we should fold the wings of our intellects and open the doors of our hearts. In other words, we should listen.

She defines prayer as "simply union with God." We do not need words when we pray, just as people in love communicate in nonverbal ways with each other. The goal for our lives, she writes, is union with God. But in order to attain that, we must have union with each other. Our progress in knowing God is correlated with our capacity to love each other. We need, she said, to follow the rhythm of solitude and action that we see in Christ's life. The contemplative and active lives cannot be separated. Both are essential to living the gospel.

An authentic poustinik, one who lives in a poustinia, is available to others and drops everything at the knock on the door. Holy people do attract others. When one is clearly conscious of the presence of God in one's heart, that person will be a light to the world. A poustinik can be flexible because he or she lives in the freedom of Christ and seeks Christ in other people. Being hospitable does not mean that we need to let people waste our time with trivialities, but we do need to be aware that the person knocking on the door may be Christ in another person.

Going into a poustinia means emptying ourselves. The main obstacle that stands between ourselves and God is self-will, and emptying ourselves of that can be painful. There may be nothing left. The emptying process involves entering the dark night. When we surrender ourselves to God we do not know what is going to happen. Letting go is not something done easily or quickly. In this connection she makes a distinction between interiorization and introspection. Introspection is looking at ourselves and all those things we think we are. Interiorization is letting God comes to us, opening ourselves to the presence. The poustinia can be the site of a terrible struggle between our desire to direct and arrange our lives and God's will for us.

In Chapter Twelve of *Poustinia*, Catherine Doherty describes some of her experiences in the poustinia listening for a word from God. Over the course of time she received many words: defenselessness, forgiveness, transparency, poverty, compassion, and others. She would describe the process of receiving the word and then her growing understanding of what it meant.

One word she received, for example, was faith. On this occasion she had spent the day at her poustinia and, although she enjoyed the day very much, no particular word came to her. She relaxed, read a little, lay in the warm sun, and swam in the river. She slept. Finally, around seven in the evening a word began to form, and she found herself thinking about the word "faith." It was certainly not a new word, but on this particular occasion it stood out. She realized, she said, as she had never understood before, that faith is a gift of God. God passionately wants to give it to us, but we must ask for it. It is a gift that allows us to enter the dark night which everyone faces from time to time. When we turn our faces to God in faith and God's eyes meet ours, the day becomes more luminous, the barriers between God and ourselves begin to disappear, and it seems that we can almost reach out and touch God.

Poustinia is more than a place. It is "a state of contemplating God in silence." Ultimately, the poustinia is within us, and we are forever immersed in the silence of God, listening to the divine word.

Periodic withdrawal to listen to God is important for everyone trying to live the gospel. Such listening may be painful, but Catherine Doherty urges us to develop the spirit of simplicity in our lives. The experience of silence and solitude may bring recognition of the word God has for us.

SUMMARY

Solitude is not easy for most people. Aelred and Doherty give us some suggestions on how to make it profitable.

Aelred of Rievaulx

1. Pray the canonical hours, the psalms.
2. Practice times of silence.

3. Alternate work, reading, and prayer. When one becomes a burden, change to another.
4. Pray briefly, but often.
5. Fast regularly.
6. Satisfy hunger without satisfying the appetite.
7. Examine your conscience at the end of the day.
8. Meditate on the life of Christ, your present condition, and your future hope.

Catherine de Hueck Doherty

1. Know that silence leads to contemplation.
2. True silence is listening to God.
3. Spend time in a poustinia on a regular basis.
4. Listen for a word from God.
5. Prepare in advance for solitude by calming the mind, closing the intellect, and opening the heart.
6. Enter solitude knowing that you are in the mind of God.
7. Empty the self.

RULES FOR WRITING
A PERSONAL PRAYER BOOK

In chapter 2 we noted that some people's discipline included putting together personal prayer books to guide them through the week. Composing and collecting prayers for your own use might be a very valuable project. Even if you think prayer should be spontaneous, recording the essence of spontaneous prayers might help stimulate your prayer in the dry periods. There is no need to require elegance of language of yourself. Simple prayers might be best. You may not even need to compose prayers in complete sentences; simply listing topics for prayer would be useful.

No collection of prayers should ever be final. Revision and new entries should be encouraged. However, favorite prayers that help you get into the act of prayer have great value. Also, collecting prayers from other people and sources that you find particularly useful is a good idea. In time you might build up a rich collection of prayers that help you get started, after which you pray more spontaneously.

Let us return to two people have previously met, Lancelot Andrewes and John Wesley. We have already learned something of their discipline of prayer, how many times they prayed and what some of their topics were. Now we will take a look at some examples from the personal prayer books they put together in the hope that these might inspire our own efforts.

LANCELOT ANDREWES

How did Andrewes approach daily prayer? Basically, he prepared prayers for morning and evening as well as prayers for each day of the week.

The Order for matins or morning prayer had three sections:

litany;

confession;

commendation.

Each section constituted two or three pages. The litany was a prayer of awakening: "Glory to Thee who givest me sleep to recruit my weakness and to remit the toils of this fretful flesh. To this day and all days, a perfect, holy, peaceful, healthy, sinless course, Vouchsafe O Lord." The litany continued, asking for a guardian angel, pardon for sin, peace for the world, repentance and strictness of life, and a good Christian death.

The confession is filled with biblical phrases: "I smite on my breasts and say with the Publican, God be merciful to me a sinner." "Lord, if Thou wilt, Thou canst make me clean; Lord, only say the word, and I shall be cleansed." There is a prayer that God will look upon Andrewes as "Thou didst look upon Magdalene at the feast, Peter in the hall, the thief on the wood." The bishop was hard on himself, whom he described as "an unclean worm, a dead dog, a putrid corpse," but also as "the work of thine own hands."

The commendation is a general prayer for the day. It

begins with a statement of praise, "Blessed art Thou, O Lord, who turnest the shadow of death into the morning and lightenest the face of the earth." Once again, the phraseology is biblical. Andrewes prayed that he might "walk soberly, holily, honestly, as in the day" and that he might "keep this day without sin." He asked that he be delivered from "the snare of the hunter and from the noisome pestilence," that his days not "be spent in vanity, nor my years in sorrow," that God "shew Thou me the way that I should walk in, for I lift up my soul unto Thee." He prayed that he be led into the "land of righteousness," that "foolish imaginations" be taken away from him, that he not listen to "undisciplined words." He wanted a watch kept over his mouth and his words "seasoned with salt." Near the end of this section he prayed that God would "guard us without failing, and place us immaculate in the presence of Thy glory in that day." Finally, he requested, "Shew some token upon me for good, that they who hate me may see it and be ashamed, because Thou, Lord, has holpen me and comforted me."

The order of evening prayer is similar in structure but the prayers are appropriate for the ending of the day. Its main sections are:

meditation;

confession;

commendation.

The meditation begins, "The day is gone, and I give Thee thanks, O Lord." Not only was it evening for the day, but Andrewes was mindful of the evening of life and prayed, "Cast me not away in the time of age; forsake me not when my strength faileth me." Day is gone and so is life going. Death comes as night comes. So Andrewes prayed "for the close of our life, that Thou wouldest direct it in peace, Christian, acceptable, sinless, shameless, and, if it please Thee, painless, Lord, O Lord." Making still heavy use of biblical language, Andrewes wrote, "By night I lift up my hands in the sanctuary, and praise the Lord. The Lord hath granted His loving-kindness in the day time: and in the night season did I sing of Him." He wanted his prayer to rise to God "as the incense, and let the lifting up of my hands be an evening sacrifice."

The confession asked for forgiveness for sins committed during the day. Andrewes said, "Evening by evening I will return in the innermost marrow of my soul: and my soul out of the deep crieth unto Thee. I have sinned, O Lord," There is no mention of specific sins, even of categories of sins, but the prayer is highly emotional: "I repent, help Thou my impenitence." He called upon God to "Remit the guilt, heal the wound, blot out the stains, clear away the same, rescue the tyranny, and make me not a public example."

Finally, the commendation is a series of prayers for the night. "To my weariness, O Lord, vouchsafe Thou rest, to my exhaustion renew Thou my strength." There is a request for "wisdom in the visions of the night," and a prayer that God not "let me in my dreams imagine what may anger Thee, what may defile me. Let not my loins be filled with illusions." He wanted to be "rid of all imaginations fleshly and satanical." At the end of the day Andrewes prayed, "Into Thy hands, O Lord, I commend myself, my spirit, soul, and body," and a request that God would "Guard my lying down and my rising up."

The longest section of the book is the Course of Prayers for the Week. Here is listed a seven-day cycle of prayer. For each day of the week there are the following:

An introduction
Confession
A Prayer for grace
Profession
Intercession
Praise

These prayers include materials from traditional liturgies, the Bible, especially the psalms, as well as Andrewes' own compositions. Each day begins with an introductory prayer. For example, the first day's introduction includes these words: "Through the tender mercies of our God the day-spring from on high hath visited us. Glory be to Thee, O Lord, glory to Thee. Creator of light, the Enlightener of the world . . . God is the Lord who hath shewed us light."

There follows each day a prayer of confession. On the seventh day, for example, Andrewes put together a number of quotations from the gospels to make this prayer: "Lord, if thou wilt, Thou canst cleanse me; Lord, only say the word, and I shall be healed. Lord, save me; Carest Thou not that we perish? Say to me, Be of good cheer, thy sins are remitted to thee. Jesu, Master, have mercy on me: Thou Son of David, Jesu, have mercy on me: Jesu, Son of David, Son of David. Lord, say to me, Ephphatha."

The next element is a prayer for grace. While these are generally petitions for the grace of God, on the fourth day Andrewes listed the traditional seven deadly sins (pride, envy, wrath, gluttony, lust, covetousness, sloth) and asked to be defended from them.

The profession is an affirmation of faith. On the second day it was the Apostles' Creed with each element precisely numbered and outlined. The profession for the third day was simply a listing of words: "Godhead, paternal love, power, providence; salvation, anointing, adoption, lordship; conception, birth, passion, cross, death, burial, descent, resurrection, ascent, sitting, return, judgment."

The fourth element in daily prayer was intercession. Andrewes prayed for various things. On the fifth day he prayed, "Let us beseech the Lord in peace, for the heavenly peace, and the salvation of our souls;—for the peace of the whole world; for the stability of God's holy Churches, and the union of them all."

Finally, the fifth part was praise. On the seventh day, he praised "the all-honourable senate of the Patriarchs, the ever-venerable band of the Prophets, the all-glorious college of the Apostles, the Evangelists, the all-illustrious army of the Martyrs, the Confessors, the assembly of Doctors, the Ascetics, the beauty of Virgins."

The final section of the *Private Devotions* consists of several brief "additional exercises." One is deprecations. Here we find prayers such as, "Deliver me from all ills and abominations of this world, from plague, famine, and war; earthquake, flood and fire, the stroke of immoderate rain and drought, blast and blight, thunder, lightning and tempest; epidemic sickness, acute and malignant, unexpected death." Forms of intercession are a listing of topics for which one might pray. For example, among the items listed are "kings, councillors, judges, nobles, soldiers, sailors, the rising generation, the possessed, the sick, orphans, foreigners, travellers, with child, in bitter bondage, overladen." There are meditations on Christian duty, on the day of judgment ("Alas, alas! woe, woe. How was I enticed by my own lust!"), and on human frailty. The final part contains some suggested meditations on holy communion.

So, we have here a liturgy for morning prayer and evening prayer, as well as prayers to be prayed each day of the week. All of the essential kinds of prayer are provided: praise, thanksgiving, confession, petition, and intercession. Rare is the person who can compose prayers of Andrewes' eloquence, but the complete nature of the content can give us guidance in the formation of our own prayers.

JOHN WESLEY

John Wesley's *A Collection of Forms of Prayer for Every Day of the Week,* 1733, was a very popular book, originally intended for his students at Oxford. It was somewhat similar to Andrewes' *Private Devotions* in that it suggested prayers for morning and evening. Like Andrewes, Wesley often used material plagiarized from other spiritual writers. The prayers for Sunday morning, for example, begin with the same language found in Lancelot Andrewes' *Private Devotions*.

> Glory be to thee, O most adorable Father, who after thou finished the work of creation, enterest into thy eternal rest.
> Glory be to thee, O holy Jesus, who, having through the eternal Spirit offered thyself a full, perfect, and sufficient sacrifice for the sins of the whole world, didst rise again the third day . . .
> Glory be to thee, O blessed Spirit, who, proceeding from the Father and the Son, didst come down in fiery tongues on the apostles . . .

The morning prayers for Sunday include a variety of petitions appropriate for the morning such as:

—that the inspiration of the Holy Spirit assist in fulfilling the duties of the day.

—that the church hear and obey the word.

—that words spoken and meditations of the heart be acceptable to God.

—that the heart may be filled with God's love.

—that the prayers and sacrifices of the church and its ministers be accepted by God.

The evening prayers appear to be more oriented toward self-examination and confession. For example, Monday evening prayer begins with confession. "Under a deep sense of my unworthiness, and with sorrow, shame, and confusion of face (I) confess I have by my manifold transgressions deserved thy severest visitations." The Tuesday evening prayer asks: "Let thy unspeakable mercy free me from the sins I have committed and deliver me from the punishment I have deserved." On Wednesday night we are to pray: "Despise not thy returning servant who earnestly begs for pardon and reconciliation."

Other themes appear in these prayers. Tuesday evening's section contains a prayer for meekness and humility: "Mortify in me the whole body of pride." The theme is expanded in Thursday evening's prayer: "When I shall be pressed to conform to the world and to the company and customs that surround me, may my answer be: I am not my own. I am not for myself, nor for the world, but for my God."

Friday morning's prayers include petitions for the mercy of Christ. They state some characteristic of Jesus followed by a plea for mercy such as:

—O Jesus, hated, calumniated, and persecuted, have

mercy upon me.

—O Jesus, betrayed and sold at a vile price, have mercy upon me.

—O Jesus, insulted, mocked, and spit upon, have mercy upon me.

—O Jesus, hanging on the accursed tree, bowing the head, giving up the ghost, have mercy upon me.

There are some petitions characteristic of Wesley's times. Thursday evening's prayers include: "Preserve and defend all Christian princes, especially our Sovereign and his family." But Wesley also prayed: "Shower down thy graces on all my relations, on all my friends and all that belong to this family." The condition of the church was much on Wesley's mind as seen in Saturday evening's prayer: "Reform the corruptions and heal the breaches of thy holy Church." Some of the prayers are taken straight from traditional liturgies such as a doxology included in Saturday evening's prayers, "Holy, holy, holy, is the Lord of hosts! Heaven and earth are full of his glory! Glory be to thee, O Lord most high."

The closing prayers for each evening include such thoughts as Tuesday's prayer, "Make me remember thee on my bed and think upon thee when I am waking. Thou has preserved me from all the dangers of the day past. Under the shadow of thy wings let me pass this night in comfort and peace." Saturday night's prayers conclude with: "Give us in thy due time a happy resurrection and a glorious rest at thy right hand forevermore."

Developing our own prayer books for morning and evening prayer would be a fine way to organize our own prayer lives. Andrewes and Wesley have given us good examples of how to organize such a book as well as the kinds of things we might want to include.

As mentioned earlier, such compositions should never be seen as final. Our growth through the various stages of spiritual development will produce different kinds and qualities of prayer. I would suggest using some kind of loose leaf notebook in which pages can easily be replaced or reorganized. For those properly equipped in our high tech society, prayers can easily be stored and retrieved in a computer. However we do it, the discipline of thoughtfully composing prayers and organizing them topically for use at appropriate times can be a valuable practice.

SUMMARY

Writing one's own personal prayer book is no easy task. Such productions should evolve over a long period of time. Constant revision is appropriate in light of new experiences. Below is a summary outline of the ideas of Andrewes and Wesley.

Lancelot Andrewes

1. Morning Prayer.
   a. Litany—a prayer of awakening.
   b. Confession.
   c. Commendation—a general prayer for the day.
2. Evening Prayer.
   a. Meditation—prayer for the evening of the day and the evening of life.
   b. Confession of sins committed during the day.
   c. Commendation—prayers for the night.

3. Prayers for each day of the week:
   a. Introductory prayer.
   b. Confession.
   c. A prayer for grace.
   d. Profession—an affirmation of faith.
   e. Intercessions.
   f. Praise.

John Wesley

1. Morning Prayer:
   a. Praise.
   b. Petitions.
2. Evening Prayer:
   a. Self-examination.
   b. Confession.
   c. Petitions.

RULES FOR LIVING

One of the basic principles of Christian spirituality is that there is a connection between living and praying. While we would hope that our prayer life would impact upon our living, it is clear from experience that the way we live impacts our prayer. We cannot live irresponsibly and immorally and expect prayer to be fruitful.

In this chapter we will look at what two monastic rules have to say about living. This may seem strange to many readers since there is a common perception that monks and nuns do not know much about living in the world and devote all of their time to prayer. However, a monastery is a community and has all of the human problems that any community experiences. Any monk or nun living an enclosed life will tell you that people who are not good at relating to others will never make it in the monastic life.

We have already seen one of these rules, the *Rule* of St. Benedict. The other is the rule of an ecumenical monastery in France called Taize, one of the few successful monastic efforts involving Protestants.

BENEDICT

We noted that Benedict believed that in the monastery the love of Christ should come before all else.

Surely that is true for us as well.

Chapter 4 of Benedict's *Rule* is titled, "The Tools for Good Works." Such tools include the commandments to love God and neighbor; not to kill, commit adultery, steal, covet, or bear false witness; to honor everyone and practice the Golden Rule. We are told to renounce ourselves in order to follow Christ. We are to love fasting. We are to look after the poor and help the troubled. Various quotations from the Bible are used instructing us not to repay evil with evil, to love our enemies, endure persecution for the sake of justice, place our hope in God alone, and fear the day of judgment. Benedict advised us to listen to holy reading, to devote ourselves to prayer, to confess our sins daily, to avoid gratifying the promptings of the flesh, to settle disputes with people before the day ends, and never to lose hope in the mercy of God. These, then, are what Benedict called "the tools of the spiritual craft."

One of the features of Benedictine life was hospitality, and every monastery had a guest house. The important point for us was the attitude toward guests. In Chapter 53 of the *Rule* we are told to welcome guests as if they were Christ, for Jesus said: "I was a stranger and you welcomed me." Benedict added that we ought to exercise special care in receiving the poor because in them "more particularly Christ is received." The rich already command a special respect. If we would regard others as Christ in our midst, we would see a new dimension in human relationships.

Benedict regarded his *Rule* as instruction for beginners, not the last word. For those seeking the perfection of the monastic life, he advised reading the Old and New Testaments, the writings and lives of the church fathers, and other rules. He called these "tools for the cultivation of virtue." Benedict recognized an important truth, that we never stop growing in our faith. There is always more to learn and our relationship with God can always be explored more deeply.

The *Rule* of St. Benedict emphasizes that discipline is important for spiritual growth. While the regulations for living in a monastery might not apply to our own lives, some of the basic concepts do. Developing a rhythm of prayer and work in our lives, the cultivation of virtue as the seed bed for prayer, using the psalms as a basis of prayer, treating each other as Christ, and striving to grow beyond our present state of spiritual attainment, are all principles that we can incorporate into our own personal rules for life.

THE RULE OF TAIZE

The monastery of Taize in France is one of the unique ecumenical institutions in the world. It was founded by Roger Schutz, who, as a Swiss university student, organized a student group for service and the study of questions of faith. The group held colloquia and retreats which included meditation, examination of conscience, and confession. In 1940 Schutz bought a house in unoccupied France in the village of Taize. Although it was intended to be a retreat center, its purpose soon changed. For two years he provided aid and shelter for refugees from Nazism and helped them escape across the Swiss border. In 1942 the Nazis occupied the house and Schutz had to remain in Switzerland while completing a dissertation. With three other students he made a temporary commitment to celibacy and communal living. They gathered for common prayer each morning and evening. Meanwhile Schutz completed a dissertation asserting that one could live a monastic life and still be faithful to the gospel.

After the war Schutz and his group returned to Taize and a community began to form. What developed was a Protestant monastery devoted to Christian unity. One of the few Protestant monasteries in the world, Taize has had enormous influence. Brothers have worked all over the world, meeting human need and promoting the idea of unity. In the summer thousands of young people have camped on the monastery grounds for renewal, challenge, and prayer.

Monasteries have always lived by a rule, and Roger Schutz developed one for Taize. *The Rule of Taize* is a simple document, describing both one's personal prayer as well as community living. The Preamble states what is a theme of this whole book, that one lives by a rule only for the sake of living the gospel and being faithful to Christ. We are encouraged to gain control over our own lives in order to make ourselves more available. Self-denial is not practiced for its own sake, but only to enable us to live the gospel. There is always a tension between our freedom and our fallen nature, and the *Rule* is designed to help us cope with that. The Preamble concludes with a number of brief but important admonitions. We should be a sign of joy and love among others. We should be present to the time in which we live and adapt ourselves to the condition of the moment. We should love the dispossessed and those suffering from injustice, as well as our neighbors whatever their political or religious beliefs. Finally, we should never accept the scandal of the separation of Christ. We should be consumed with a zeal for the unity of the church.

While the *Rule* prescribes community life, it also

contains a discussion of the individual's interior life. The Taize community has common prayer three times a day in services that are very impressive to visitors. Such common prayer was described as "the communion of saints." To be such, however, requires intercession for the church and for other people. Beneath the surface of this common worship is some of the invisible reality of God's kingdom. The robes worn by the monks at prayer were to remind them that their whole being must be clothed by Christ.

However, the *Rule* does not dispense any members from developing their own personal prayer lives. Personal and community prayer sustain each other. Personal prayer involves surrendering ourselves to the word of God, taking possession of us.

Anyone who tries to pray knows that we are often distracted and our attention wanders. We should turn to prayer as soon as we notice this distraction, believing that Christ is present within us. When we cannot offer our minds to God, we can at least offer our bodies, since our presence in prayer signifies our desire to praise God.

The *Rule* suggests that there should be a connection between our work and the word of God. Our prayer becomes total when it is one with our work.

Interior silence is essential to our life in Christ, because it makes possible our conversation with him. Such silence requires forgetting ourselves, quieting discordant voices, and overcoming obsessive worry. We often fear such silence and would rather stay busy with work in order to avoid it. However, silence is required for dialogue, for intimacy with Jesus Christ. Perfect joy, says the *Rule,* is laying aside of self in peaceful love.

The *Rule* calls for simplicity of life as a way of avoiding those complications which lead to evil. We are advised to cast off useless burdens, to admit our mistakes with simplicity, and to forsake the obsession with our own progress or failure, in order to fix our gaze on Christ.

Finally, the *Rule* encourages us to practice mercy. Being at peace with Christ implies living in peace with our neighbor. We are reminded that Jesus taught forgiving another seventy times seven. We must be prepared at all times to forgive each other, to avoid a tendency to give in to personal dislikes, to judge another when that person is having a bad day. We should not engage in petty controversies nor listen to insinuations about others. When we live in mercy we avoid both susceptibility and disappointment. The ideal is to live simply in self-forgetfulness, be joyful, and expect nothing in return.

Other elements in the *Rule* deal with the community life of the monastery, and are not particularly relevant for us. However, the spirit of the *Rule* of Taize can apply to any Christian. To live simply, to pray regularly, and to be merciful, would produce fine Christian character.

SUMMARY

The connection between living and praying may be the most overlooked dimension of prayer. The basic rule for living, of course, is the gospel. The rules of St. Benedict and the Taize community, however, give us guidance on living in the context of a life of prayer. These rules are not easily summarized, but below is a list of relevant points.

The Rule of St. Benedict

1. The tools of good works:
    a. The Ten Commandments.

   b. The Golden Rule.

   c. To renounce the self.

   d. To love fasting.

   e. To look after the poor and help the troubled.

   f. To love enemies and endure persecution.

   g. To fear the day of judgment.

   h. To listen to (or to do) holy reading.

   i. To pray.

   j. To confess sins.

   k. To avoid gratifying the flesh.

   l. To settle disputes before the day ends.

  m. Never to lose hope in the mercy of God.

2. Practice hospitality.
3. Read the Bible and the church fathers.
4. Develop a rhythm of prayer and work.
5. Treat each other as Christ.

The Rule of Taize

1. Practice self-control and self-denial.
2. Be a sign of joy and love to others.
3. Love the dispossessed and those suffering injustice.
4. Have a zeal for the unity of the church.
5. Practice common prayer three times a day.
6. Practice personal prayer.
7. Have interior silence.
8. Practice simplicity of life.
9. Practice mercy and avoid judgment.

9

RULES FOR SPIRITUAL GROWTH

One of the basic purposes of any rule we may adopt or design for ourselves is to foster our growth in the knowledge of God. There will be times when we will feel surges of progress and new insight. There will be others when we will wonder if we are making any headway at all or, indeed, if we are regressing. Spiritual growth produces times of illumination as well as times of confusion. When we sense that progress is being made, we may be on the brink of a dry period, and when we seem to be wandering in darkness and disorientation we may actually be closest to God. Throughout the history of Christian spirituality many have plotted the course for us, pointed out the milestones, and anticipated the next stations on the journey. Let us take a look at five such writers, two of whom we have already met.

GUIGO II

One of the truly delightful little books to come out of the twelfth century was a brief treatise called *The Ladder of Monks.* Its author is known to us by the name, Guigo II, but we know little of the man. He was the prior of a Carthusian monastery, located in the Alps, a few miles north of Grenoble. There is a legend that after his death so many healings occurred over his grave that huge throngs of pilgrims disrupted the life of the monastery. The Prior had to command the departed Guigo to stop producing miracles.

The Ladder of Monks lists four progressive activities for spiritual growth. The first rung on the ladder is the *reading* of scripture. After we have read a passage and noticed that there might be more meaning that what we immediately see on the surface, we ascend to the second rung which is *meditation*. This involves pondering the passage we have read, turning it over in our minds and trying to draw deeper meaning from it. Meditation leads us to the third rung, *prayer*. Having read and meditated on the passage we are moved to pray about it, asking God to help us attain for our lives the point the passage teaches. Finally, we ascend to the fourth rung of the ladder, which is *contemplation*. At this stage, God, responding to our reading, meditation, and prayer, comes to meet us and fulfills our longing for the divine presence.

This is a very simple little scheme which emphasizes the progressive nature of spiritual activity. Normally, we do not expect an instant vision of God, but by the development of our spiritual faculties, we grow toward the knowledge of the divine.

BONAVENTURE

A classic scheme that we find in much of the literature of Christian spirituality was explained by a second generation Italian Franciscan of the thirteenth century named Bonaventure, in a little book called *The Triple Way*. Among his other books is his order's official biography of St. Francis of Assisi and a classic on mystical theology, *The Mind's Road to God.*

The Triple Way outlines our spiritual growth through three stages: purgation, illumination, and union with God. *Purgation* is the stage in which we rid our lives of those elements that obscure the vision of God. This may mean changing our values, our life-styles, our attitudes, even our possessions. The second stage, *illumination,* means that we learn more about God, we have a clearer grasp of the divine mysteries, the gospel becomes clearer to us. The final stage, *union,* however, is not just a matter of knowing about God, it is a matter of oneness, of intimacy, with God. Once again we see the progressive nature of our quest. The first stage involves living, the second involves knowing, and the third is losing ourselves in the vision of God.

IGNATIUS LOYOLA

In the sixteenth century, while the Protestant Reformation was taking place in Germany, Switzerland, and other European countries, a major movement for spiritual renewal was originating in the Catholic Church in Spain. Among the leaders it produced was the founder of the Jesuit Order, a young nobleman named Ignatius Loyola. He developed a system of meditation called the *Spiritual Exercises*. Designed for a four-week retreat with meditations for each week, the system became widely used. At the end of the book is a set of "Guidelines for the Discernment of Spirits." These tell us how to know when we have received spiritual consolations; in other words, how to know when we are making progress.

Ignatius said, in essence, that we are making progress when we feel inflamed with a love for God and, as a result, we have no love for created things on earth except through the One who created them. Another sign is when we are moved to tears because of our love for Christ, our sorrow for our sins, and our response to the passion of Christ. Finally, we are growing as Christians when we experience an increase in faith, hope and love, and when we have an interior joy that quiets our souls and brings peace in God.

Ignatius warned us in these guidelines that evil often comes to us in the appearance of good, bringing us good and holy thoughts, but subtly drawing us away from God. We should not mistake this for progress.

Here we have reconfirmed the idea that the measure of authentic spirituality is what it produces in our lives.

EVELYN UNDERHILL

We have already met Evelyn Underhill, a British writer of the first half of the twentieth century. In her massive study, *Mysticism,* she expands upon Bonaventure's outline of spiritual growth. After studying the major figures in the history of Christian mysticism, she concluded that almost everyone moves through five stages of growth.

The first is our awakening to an *awareness* of a divine reality. This awakening may be sudden or gradual, but it means that we realize that there is another level of reality beyond what we immediately perceive with our senses. As a result, we begin to reorder our lives so that we might know and experience this Reality, or God, if you prefer to use that term. This second stage corresponds to Bonaventure's *purgation*. We attempt to get rid of those things that inhibit our knowledge of God. This leads to the third stage, *illumination*. Now we are operating on a new level of perception. We have a new awareness of God, far beyond what we previously thought was possible. It would appear that we have reached the goal of our quest, a knowledge of God far deeper and more intimate that we ever knew before. We are overwhelmed by divine mystery.

However it is at just this point that we are most vulnerable to the next stage which, borrowing a phrase from St. John of the Cross, she called the *dark night of the soul*. All of the progress we have made seems to be lost. We find ourselves lethargic and frustrated. We try to pray and we cannot settle down. We are distracted by restlessness. There is a loss of what we thought was the presence of God in our lives and a loss of will to continue the quest. This is the most dangerous point in our journey because the temptation to give up is very strong. However, this stage is part of the purgation process, a self-purification. It passes when we finally surrender ourselves to God and move into the fifth stage, *the unitive life*. Underhill called this stage "humanity's top note," and said that those who have reached this point live at "transcendent levels of reality." A wide variety of terms is used to describe this union: spiritual marriage, self-surrender, freedom, unification of personality, deification, the beatific vision, mystic joy. Suffice it to say for now that we are talking about a condition of deepest intimacy with God, the clearest awareness of the divine, the union of our will and God's will.

This does not happen overnight, but is prepared for by awareness, purgation, illumination, and the purification of the dark night experience. Where are you in this process?

THOMAS MERTON

Finally, let us turn again to Thomas Merton whom we met in chapter 3. There we looked at his book, *Contemplative Prayer*. Another important book he wrote was *New Seeds of Contemplation*, which appeared in 1961. You might find it a good source to study in a small church group.

He suggested in this volume that most people do not experience God's presence in a sudden flash, but by very gradual, almost imperceptible steps. Without solid groundwork we will probably never experience contemplative prayer. In fact, he said, prayer is only truly contemplative when it becomes habitual.

Many of us, he believed, arrive at the threshold of the contemplation of God without knowing it. We find ourselves in the dark night and fear that our quest has ended in failure. However, he said, the usual road to contemplation is through the desert, a barren land with no trees, beauty or water. This prospect is so frightening that we are afraid to enter. In that desert God is nowhere to be found. Yet some people sense that peace is to be found in the heart of darkness, so they keep still, they stop trying to force prayer and meditation and other spiritual exercises, and they patiently trust in God. In the midst of darkness and emptiness, God leads them to the promised land.

We must learn to abandon all of our spiritual

progress into the hands of God, said Merton. There is a time when inaction is needed. If we sense that God is drawing us to contemplation, we should remain in prayer that is simple, free of images and activity, and wait for God's will to be done. Even though we may think we are not doing anything, below the surface of consciousness the mind and will are being drawn into a deep, intense, and supernatural activity, that will later bear fruit in our lives.

The key to working through the dark night is unfailing trust in God and the courage to risk everything for God. Merton warns us that the desire for religious experiences can be a major obstacle in our quest for God. Such things offer us no lasting satisfaction. He urges us to develop spiritually mature passions which he defines as those that are "pure, clean, gentle, quiet, nonviolent, forgetful of themselves, detached and above all when they are humble and obedient to reason and grace."

All of these schemes of growth begin with activity on our part where we work hard to develop ourselves spiritually. But they end with our waiting for God and turning ourselves over to that which we seek. We begin immaturely, but as we grow and develop we put away childish things and look to that which is shrouded in mystery. It is our willingness to plunge into the unknown that makes possible the deepest intimacy with God.

SUMMARY

Spiritual growth is a process that never ends. We can always receive new knowledge, new insight, and a deeper awareness of the divine mystery. The outlines for spiritual growth presented in this chapter provide some guidance for determining where we are in our own development. Religious longings ebb and flow throughout life. We do not live on a spiritual high all of the time. When our life of prayer is not going well, these schemes can help us see where we have positioned ourselves and give directions for the next moves.

Guigo II

1. Reading
2. Meditation
3. Prayer
4. Contemplation

Bonaventure

1. Purgation—living
2. Illumination—knowing
3. Union—losing ourselves

Ignatius Loyola

1. Signs of progress:
   a. Being inflamed with a love for God.
   b. Being moved to tears because of:
      (1) our love for Christ.
      (2) sorrow for our sins.
      (3) the passion of Christ.
   c. Having an increase in faith, hope, and love.
   d. Having an interior joy that quiets the soul and brings peace in God.
2. Warning: Evil often has the appearance of good, bring us holy thoughts but subtly drawing us away from God.
3. The measure of authentic spirituality is what it produces in our lives.

Evelyn Underhill

1. Awareness of a divine reality.
2. Purgation of things that inhibit our knowledge of God.
3. Illumination, growing in our knowledge of God.
4. The dark night of the soul.
5. The unitive life

Thomas Merton

1. Many people develop a knowledge of God by slow, gradual steps.
2. Prayer is truly contemplative when it becomes habitual.
3. The usual road to contemplation is through the dark night experience when one must patiently trust God.
4. We must abandon our spiritual progress into the hands of God.
5. When sensing that God is drawing us to contemplation, we must remain in prayer that is simple, free of images, and wait upon the will of God.
6. The key to growth is unfailing trust in God.

10

DESIGNING A RULE FOR PRAYER

Now that you have seen rules and approaches to prayer by others, how will you design a rule for your own life? Your rule may be simply no more than ideas in the back of your mind. Or, it may be something you carefully write out and refer to from time to time. Whatever you do, keep your rule flexible, open to change as you grow. If a once valuable practice no longer serves any useful purpose, do not be afraid to discard it or replace it with something else. It would probably be a mistake to take any idea presented in the rules we have already studied and continue to follow it forever. For example, you may decide to pray at a certain time every morning, and for many years this practice serves you well. However, changes in your life such as age, family, employment, retirement, or health, may indicate that some other time for prayer might be more suitable. There may be times in your life when such things as fasting, solitude, or being a member of a prayer group, may be more appropriate than at other times. As you deepen your intimacy with God your theology is likely to change. Images and concepts once useful may be discarded and new ones adopted as you mature in your understanding of the gospel. Be open to change and growth.

At any point in your life, however, it may be good to have come to some conclusions about the disciplines you will practice in pursuing a life of prayer. With experience the practices will evolve and change, but you need a starting point.

As has been stated several times already, the first task in attempting to deepen a prayer life is to develop a contemplative attitude. It is not easy to be open to God's presence and sense it in everyday events. We are confronted with countless distractions that obscure our perception of the divine, and we all have a natural resistance to turning over our lives to someone else.

One way to develop a contemplative attitude is through reading scripture and the writings of those who have attained some level of intimacy with God. Beware of so-called devotional literature that knows nothing of the struggle with doubt and darkness. Spiritual growth is at times a painful process, and we can learn much from those who have been through it. Those who teach a superficial optimism and self-serving piety are teaching a faith that will crumble in crisis. There are times when life deals us hard blows and God seems remote or even nonexistent. In those situations we need a faith that has been forged in the crucible of spiritual struggle. Read those who represent the best in the Christian tradition.

So, the first element in a rule is to set aside time for reading and Bible study as a means of forming a contemplative attitude. Having a book that you are reading regularly, even if only a few pages or a few verses a day, provides continuing stimulation and nurture. Our electronic age has opened other possibilities. There are a variety of good tapes, audio and video, that can serve the same purpose as reading. In a tight schedule, listening to tapes in a car while commuting to work or while traveling can make useful what otherwise might be wasted time.

A major part of our rule, of course, will be devoted to how and when we pray. How much time is realistic for you to devote to prayer in a day? Many of the people we studied in this book said that prayer should be brief unless extended by the inspiration of the Holy Spirit. Praying briefly, but frequently, may be better than scheduling large periods of time that we can never actually devote to prayer. John Wesley's suggestion that brief prayers be prayed on the hour and collects at 9:00, noon, and 3:00 may be a little rigid for you, but the idea of sanctifying the day by brief, frequent prayer throughout it has some merit, however we decide we can do it.

Finding time for prayer is not easy in our culture. We may offer brief spontaneous prayers from time to time, but finding longer periods is difficult. Often we have to work it in between job, family life, and other responsibilities. Sometimes we may find we have to arise before the family in the morning unless, of course, we pray with the family. Or, we may have to stay up a little later at night. Chances are that our jobs will not allow any time for prayer, but we might think of those odd moments we could use: commuting on a bus, traveling on a plane, standing in line, waiting for appointments. There are many moments in life that give us brief opportunities for reading or thinking or praying.

Still, however, you may want to plan some occasions for more leisurely prayer when you can spend some calm, unrushed time in prayer. Your rule should include the different kinds of prayer we have studied: praise, adoration, thanksgiving, confession, petition, doxology. Following this outline prevents our making prayer only a self-serving act. As was suggested in chapter 7, you might try your hand at writing a few prayers for each category.

William Law, you will recall from chapter 2, suggested using a different topic for prayer at different times of the day. Praise in the morning, intercession at midday, confession in the evening, is a useful scheme if you can fit it into your schedule. A rule that will be effective must be appropriate for your personality. Some of us are morning people and some of us are night people. There is no right or wrong time to pray; it is a matter of what times work best for who we are.

A number of the people referred to in this book emphasized the importance of the examination of conscience. Many suggested doing this at the end of the day, but there is nothing sacred about that time. It is useful to evaluate the day before going to bed, but you could evaluate the previous day early in the morning.

John Wesley, in chapter 2, offered some suggestions for the sorts of questions you might ask of yourselves when examining your conscience. Luther's system of meditating on the Lord's Prayer and the Ten Commandments might be helpful. In the Old Testament psalms we find some good prayers of confession to offer. Psalms 6, 32, 38, 51, 102, 130, and 143, are traditionally regarded as penitential psalms or psalms of confession. Notice that Psalm 51, for example, does not just stop with confession. It is also a prayer for renewal. The gospel does not call upon us to feel guilty all the time. It promises new life in Jesus Christ to those who are repentant.

For many people, perhaps for you, keeping a spiritual journal, or any other kind for that matter, is a good way to reflect on one's life and where it is going. Dorothy Day, you may remember from chapter 4, said that keeping a journal was one way of praying. It is also useful in charting your spiritual growth.

Finally, on the matter of prayer, you might experiment with developing a personal prayer book such as Andrewes and Wesley had. It need not be as elaborate as theirs, but you might include a simple liturgy: the use of some psalms, the Lord's Prayer, a doxology, a scripture reading, your own prayers.

Most spiritual writers, including Bonaventure and Evelyn Underhill, as we saw in chapter 9, emphasized the purgation stage in spiritual growth. Self-denial for its own sake is of no real value. In fact, it can be harmful if it leads to spiritual pride. It would be useful, however, from time to time, to examine your values and take a look at what is really important to you in life. If your ultimate happiness depends on trivial things, things that will eventually lose their luster, some reevaluation of priorities might be in order. Most of the people described in this book were noted for the simplicity of their lives and their lack of dependence on things many of us are tempted to think are so important to us. Things in themselves are neutral; it is our attitude toward them that matters. If driving a certain kind of car, or living in a particular neighborhood, or having high status in the community is the most important thing to you, do not be surprised if God seems distant.

It might be a useful spiritual exercise for you to practice a temporary self-denial during Lent or some other time. Many people deny themselves a certain amount of food, but it could be something else. One of the most valuable benefits of such self-denial is what we learn about ourselves. We may not realize how dependent we are on certain things until we try to do without them. That is when we discover how little control we have over ourselves and what values are truly important to us. Find a point in your rule for some measure of self-denial, not to be heroic in your devotion, but to learn something about yourself.

Every personal rule should include some time of silence for intentional listening to God. It may include a day away in a poustinia as we learned in chapter 6, or it might be as simple as a solitary walk around the block or in a park. There are many retreat centers available these days, and scheduling periodic retreats, even if only once a year for two or three days, can be renewing. Churches, denominations, and other groups offer retreats, and these opportunities should be used.

So far we have been talking about solitary, interior matters. A good rule, however, should include directions on community life. Most important for many people is family life. Your rule should express a commitment to your family and its welfare. It should warn you not to neglect what may be the greatest source of love you have in this world. God is love, and whenever people love each other, God is present. It is very easy to get so caught up in one's vocation or community responsibilities, or even church life, that the family is neglected. Yet, the love your family members have for each other could be your greatest resource for spiritual growth.

For those who do not have immediate families, a circle of friends that enriches your life deserves your commitment. Everyone needs some kind of intimate community, but you will never have one unless you feel some level of responsibility to and love for it.

Dorothy Day and Dom Helder Camara, in chapter 4, emphasized the importance of seeing Christ in other people, especially in those who have less than you do. It is not easy to see the image of God in those who make your life miserable. However, we must develop the sensitivity to the divine presence in another, and intentionally looking for that ought to be part of a personal rule.

And, of course, your rule should include an involvement in the corporate worship of the church. Regular attendance, receiving the sacraments, hearing the word preached, and praying together with others, are all things to which we must be committed if we are to have a well-balanced Christian life.

The church also provides other assistance in living the gospel. It provides us with opportunities for study and service of which we ought to take advantage. Commitments to these ought also to be part of a personal rule.

Beyond that, our rule should include a commitment to the Christian community beyond our local church. As part of the church we are related to the worldwide ministry of the gospel. Understanding the rest of the world and doing what we can to promote the international ministry of the church should be important to us.

A significant part of our rule should be concerned with stewardship. I did not put this in the section on self-denial, because stewardship has a more positive dimension to it. You may well be moved to give up something once important to you in order to support a cause you think worthy. However, a grudging denial in order to give is not stewardship. Authentic stewardship is characterized by a joy in giving, by a generous spirit, by a realization of the meaning and joy that comes from giving. A spirit of giving can be very liberating and free you from some of the oppressive features of our culture. While some people find joy in having, there are others who find it in giving, in meeting a human need or causing something worthwhile to happen. Most of the people described in this book lived simple lives by choice, not because it was forced upon them. Whether it was William Law giving milk to the people in his neighborhood, Dorothy Day providing hospitality for the homeless, or Dom Helder Camara giving up an archbishop's mansion for a small room in a church, they all did it because they found joy and satisfaction in such an act. Let your own rule include a commitment to giving.

The following summary outline may serve as a checklist in designing your own rule. Perhaps some elements will not be appropriate for you, but at least give them your consideration.

A. Developing a contemplative attitude
    1. Reading scripture
    2. Reading that develops faith
B. Prayer
    1. Times
    2. Content
       a. Praise
       b. Adoration
       c. Thanksgiving
       d. Confession
       e. Petition
       f. Doxology
    3. Examination of conscience
    4. Journaling
    5. A personal prayerbook
C. Purgation
    1. Examination of values
    2. Self-denial
D. Silence
E. Community life
    1. Family or close friends

2. Seeing Christ in others
F. The church
    1. Public worship
    2. Opportunities for study and service
    3. Commitment to the worldwide ministry
G. Stewardship

I hope these suggestions will be helpful in designing your own personal rule and organizing your life. Remember, the purpose of a rule is to enable you to live the gospel. It has no value of its own. What matters is what it produces in your life. May your own rule result in greater faithfulness, deeper discipline, and the vision of God.

11

SOURCES

CHAPTER 1: RULES ON HOW TO PRAY

Calvin, John, *The Institutes of the Christian Religion.*
Volumes XX–XXI of the *Library of Christian
Classics*. Philadelphia: Westminster Press, 1960.
Cassian, John, "Conferences," *Western Asceticism.*
Volume XII of the *Library of Christian Classics.*
Philadelphia: Westminster Press, 1958.
Luther, Martin, "A Simple Way to Pray," *Luther's Works*,
Volume 48. Philadelphia: Fortress Press, 1968.
Origen, "On Prayer," *Origen.* New York: Paulist Press,
1979.

CHAPTER 2: RULES FOR MAINTAINING
A PRAYER LIFE

Andrewes, Lancelot, *The Private Devotions of Lancelot
Andrewes,* edited by John Henry Newman. New
York: Abingdon-Cokesbury, 1950.
Benedict of Nursia, *The Rule of St. Benedict in English.*
Collegeville, Minnesota: The Liturgical Press, 1982.
"The Didache," *Early Christian Fathers.* Volume I of the
Library of Christian Classics. Philadelphia:
Westminster Press, 1953.

Law, William, *A Serious Call to the Devout and Holy Life.* New York: Paulist Press, 1978.

Wesley, John, "A Scheme of Self-Examination," *John and Charles Wesley.* New York: Paulist Press, 1981.

Wesley, John, *John Wesley's Prayers.* Edited by Frederick C. Gill. New York: Abingdon-Cokesbury, 1951.

CHAPTER 3: RULES FOR DEVELOPING A CONTEMPLATIVE ATTITUDE

Merton, Thomas, *Contemplative Prayer.* New York: Herder and Herder, 1969.

Underhill, Evelyn, *Practical Mysticism.* New York: E. P. Dutton, 1915.

Underhill, Evelyn, "Prayer," *Evelyn Underhill: Modern Guide to the Ancient Quest for the Holy,* edited by Dana Green. Albany: State University of New York Press, 1988. First published as a pamphlet by the YWCA in 1926.

CHAPTER 4: RULES FOR PRAYER AND SOCIAL ACTION

Camara, Dom Helder, *Through the Gospels with Dom Helder Camara.* Maryknoll, N.Y.: Orbis Books, 1986.

Day, Dorothy, "On Pilgrimage," *The Catholic Worker.* (Regular Column)

CHAPTER 5: RULES FOR PRAYER IN CRISIS

Bonhoeffer, Dietrich, *Life Together.* New York: Harper and Row, 1954.

Bonhoeffer, Dietrich, *Prisoner for God: Letters and Papers from Prison*. New York: Macmillan, 1953.

King, Martin Luther, Jr., *Stride Toward Freedom*. New York: Harper and Row, 1958.

King, Martin Luther, Jr., *Why We Can't Wait*. New York: Harper and Row, 1963.

CHAPTER 6: RULES FOR SOLITUDE

Aelred of Rievaulx, "Rule of Life for a Recluse," *The Works of Aelred of Rievaulx,* Volume 1. Spencer, Massachusetts: Cistercian Publications, 1971.

Doherty, Catherine de Hueck, *Poustinia*. Notre Dame, Indiana: Ave Maria Press, 1975.

CHAPTER 7: RULES FOR WRITING A PERSONAL PRAYER BOOK

Andrewes, Lancelot (see chapter 2).

Wesley, John (see chapter 2).

CHAPTER 8: RULES FOR PRAYER AND LIVING

Benedict (see chapter 2).

The Rule of Taize. New York: Seabury Press, 1968.

CHAPTER 9: RULES FOR SPIRITUAL GROWTH

Bonaventure, "The Triple Way," *The Works of St. Bonaventure.* Volume I. Patterson, N.J.: St. Anthony Guild Press, 1960.

Guigo II, *The Ladder of Monks and Twelve Meditations*. Kalamazoo: Cistercian Publications, 1981.

Ignatius Loyola, *The Spiritual Exercises: A Literal Translation and a Contemporary Reading*. St. Louis: Institute of Jesuit Sources, 1978.

Merton, Thomas, *New Seeds of Contemplation*. New York: New Directions, 1961.

Underhill, Evelyn, *Mysticism*. New York: E. P. Dutton, 1930.